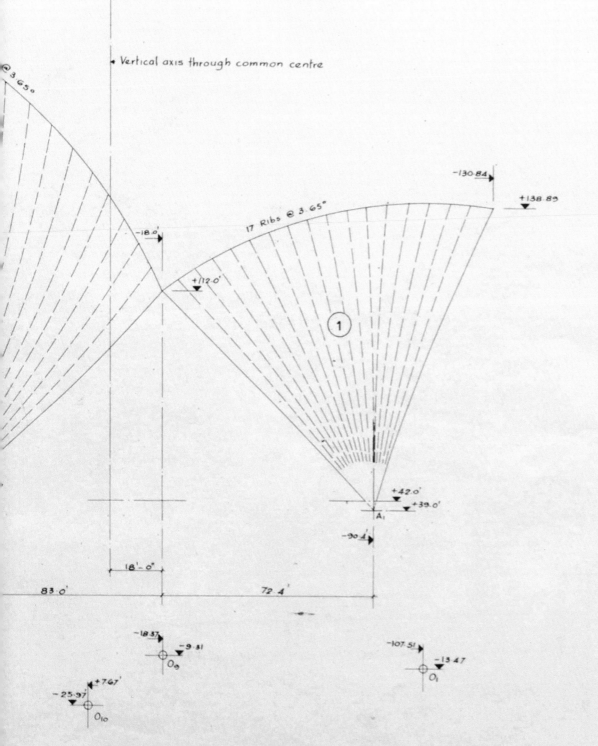

Vertical axis through common centre

@ 3.65°

17 Ribs @ 3.65°

−130.84

+138.89

−18.0'

+112.0'

①

+42.0'
+39.0'

A₁

−90.4'

18'−0"

83.0'

72.4'

−18.37
−9.31
O₉

−107.51
−13.47
O₁

+7.67'
−25.97
O₁₀

Total Design over time

ARUP

Cover image: wooden model
showing a geometrical solution for
the Sydney Opera House shells.

End papers: plans for Sydney
Opera House roof elevation, from
Arup archive.

Foreword
Gregory Hodkinson

Engineering is central to human progress – almost nothing is invented without it – and Ove Arup was an extraordinary engineer who was deeply concerned with that progress. His vision for the role of engineering in design and of design in engineering was shaped by humanistic, rather than simply technical, principles. This breadth of vision has inspired generations to pursue the art and science of Total Design in the firm he started at age 51 in 1946.

The purpose of the firm founded by Ove has remained constant over the ensuing 70 years. The results of his admonition to expand its field of activity into adjoining fields, solely in the quest for overall quality, has produced the broadening body of work across the world that is sampled in this volume.

In his latter years Ove was concerned with the impact of design at both small and large scale and the future we are effectively designing for humanity on our planet. If he were with us today I think he would recognise the pursuit of quality and the social purpose of design in the current work of the firm. I very much hope and fully expect they will be recognised in the work of the firm that is his legacy 70 years and more hence.

Gregory Hodkinson
Arup Group Chairman

Contents

Preface
Engineering a better world

When it comes to creativity and the arts, the worlds of design, fashion and architecture tend to grab our attention. But when we look a little closer to appreciate the wonderful façade on our favourite building, the performance of a car, or the mysterious ease with which something 'just works', often what we are admiring is the work of the engineer.

It is their work that not only interprets and brings a vision to life, but frequently has a formative hand in its design. And yet, we rarely acknowledge the technical brilliance behind the artistic or architectural expression.

At its heart, engineering is about helping people live simpler, easier lives. Its social dimension affects our quality of life, whether it is a new transport route that shortens a daily commute by an hour or two, or the building of a bridge that will connect an isolated rural community to the world beyond.

In this environment, Ove Arup and his firm stand out. Ove's progressive ideas about shaping a better world make him the perfect lens through which to show that creative engineering is about more than nuts and bolts and screws.

His holistic approach – realised in his Total Design philosophy – has stood the test of time. And it will continue to be relevant as the world changes. Innovations such as artificial intelligence, autonomous driving and leaps in communication will all require engineering to make the complex simple.

Britain has a great engineering tradition: from Matthew Boulton in the 18th century and Isambard Kingdom Brunel in the 19th century, to James Dyson today. Since the V&A's beginnings, design and engineering have been a significant part of the museum's purpose. We have often marvelled at engineers' impressive feats – incredible underground networks, complex airports, magnificent bridges – but we want to show that engineering is about much more than this.

By focusing on engineering through a book that celebrates its achievements and looks to the future, we can see how profoundly it impacts your daily life. Engineering is so important to the world we live in. We should give it the recognition – and respect – it deserves.

Martin Roth
Director of the Victoria and Albert Museum

Ove Arup

From the Sydney Opera House to Centre Pompidou and High Speed 1, Arup, the firm Ove created in 1946, is an influential force in design and engineering. The principles of Total Design, which he put in place, were revolutionary for their day. They are as relevant now as they were when he started out some 70 years ago.

Sydney Opera House, Australia
The construction of the opera house propelled Arup onto a global stage. Design began in the 1950s – and Ove turned a bold concept into a reality. The complex design work for the iconic pre-cast concrete shells was achieved through pioneering use of computers to model the roof and analyse the structure. Since the opera house opened in 1973, Arup has continued to work on upgrades and refurbishments.

90°
The bridge was constructed in two halves that were simply rotated 90° to meet in the middle.

Sir Ove Arup, 1895–1988.

The influence of Ove Arup

Ove Arup was arguably one of the greatest civil engineers of the 20th century.

Ove's education was broad and privileged. Above all, it was underpinned by his formidable intellect. After school, he studied philosophy for three years. This philosophical education was to have a seminal influence on his chosen career as a civil engineer. He had an insatiable, enquiring mind, and developed a deep interest in art and architecture. It was no surprise that during the 1920s and 1930s, he was attracted to contemporary architecture and the practitioners of what became known as the Modern Movement. This led to a lifelong passion for harnessing and furthering the integration of the burgeoning technologies associated with construction in producing great and socially useful architecture.

His ability to articulate the necessity for this integration – for a more creative collaboration between architects and technical specialists – became a cornerstone of his increasing fame. Initially, this argument was associated with the obvious influence of structure on architecture, but later embraced all the

Kingsgate Bridge, Durham, UK
This 1963 elegant concrete bridge over the River Wear connects Durham University's 19th century buildings on the cathedral peninsula to the expanding campus south of the river. It is the last project Ove designed himself. He described it as an example of "the complete integration of architecture, structure and method of construction".

Beautifully designed
When the two halves of the bridge met in the middle of the river, a movement joint was required. Ove made the joint a part of the architecture rather than hiding it. This beautiful detail is made of a 'T' that points to the town and a 'U' for the university side, with two cylinders between them to allow the movement.

technologies that go into construction. He repeatedly said that it seemed to him to be all so obvious. Others soon followed talking about it, but Ove led by example and practised what he preached.

At the turn of the century, *New Civil Engineer*, the weekly news magazine for the civil engineering industry, carried out a poll among its readers asking who was the most influential figure of the profession in the 20th century. Ove Arup headed the poll by a large margin.

His influence was largely supported and spread by the firm he created. He proudly and repeatedly said that initially he chose all his collaborators personally. There was no recognisable method in his selection process. He didn't care about gender, race, colour or even academic achievement. He simply wanted to get a feel as to the type of person he was hiring and whether or not he or she would fit in with his, then unstated, aims and objectives. This personal selection process inevitably stopped when the firm grew to more than a few dozen people. But it created the basis for a flat organisational structure. Once he had chosen his colleagues and employees, Ove let go of   >

Penguin Pool, London Zoo, UK
With its daring spiral ramp, the pool, unveiled in
1934, was one of the first structures to use reinforced
concrete. Its playful form mimics the penguins' natural
habitat. Only through close collaboration between the
designer, engineer, architect and builder could such an
outrageous structure be conceived in this material. The
project established the reputations of Ove Arup and
Tecton, the architectural firm led by Berthold Lubetkin.

the reins and placed an almost childlike trust in them. He delegated responsibility quite naturally. The astonishing success of Arup the firm is a consequence of its founder's liberal leadership, which gave his collaborators almost unlimited responsibility to further the fortunes of the firm. It also resulted in many members of Arup being given opportunities to further their careers, which in some instances proved to be stellar.

The development of the firm he created took place in the context of this liberal and often chaotic leadership, but within an evolving and not yet formally articulated set of values and principles. In 1970, a meeting was convened which was attended by all the leaders of Arup, both from the UK and from abroad. The objective of the meeting was to discuss the future, particularly the consequences of the inevitable ageing of Ove and his original partners. We wanted to examine how the growing firm could be seamlessly handed on to future generations. Ove was asked to open the proceedings.

He produced a paper, subsequently called 'The Key Speech'. For the first time, and in his own idiosyncratic and brilliant manner, he set out the values and objectives that we were practising but that had so far not been comprehensively articulated. It was simply a statement of the quest for excellence in the context of decent, honourable and responsible behaviour. This 'Key Speech' has become the firm's mantra. It has stood the test of time and is now the basis on which the 13,500 members of Arup conduct themselves. >

Mulberry Harbour, UK
During World War II, Ove worked on designs for temporary portable harbours to facilitate the Allied invasion of Normandy. Together with Ronald Jenkins, he was responsible for a new type of concrete fender. Jenkins later became Ove's senior partner at Ove Arup & Partners.

Brynmawr Rubber Factory, UK
Working as a consultant instead of
a builder's engineer, Ove was able to
show his command of highly delicate
reinforced concrete shell structures.
The centrepiece of the Welsh factory
complex was the 4,400m² roof,
supported on only four internal columns
made up of nine concrete shell domes,
each a mere 76mm thick.

Ove's greatness was enhanced by his being a
key influence in creating the employee-oriented
ownership structure of the firm. While he was not the
progenitor of the scheme, he embraced it generously
and wholeheartedly. This devolution of ownership has
proved to be the keystone to the firm's success and could
not have been achieved without Ove's total commitment.

Ove always wanted a small firm where everyone
knew each other and in which there was a warm family
atmosphere. However, he realised, albeit reluctantly, that
one of the consequences of unlimited delegation, coupled
with his now well-publicised ideas on professional
collaboration, would inevitably be growth. He would
probably be heartened that the aspirations of the firm,
which he articulated so eloquently, were being embraced
and passed on from generation to generation.

Sir Jack Zunz, January 2016
Principal structural designer of the Sydney Opera House
and former chairman of Ove Arup & Partners.

Jack Zunz, left, and Ove Arup.

Hidden hand of the engineer

The engineer is like a magician. In buildings of all kinds, people concentrate on the activities they are there to do. Yet behind the scenes every aspect has been considered – from security and lighting to air conditioning and climate control – to ensure the user experience is enhanced without being interrupted. This is especially true for cultural buildings, galleries and concert halls where the sensory environment makes a crucial contribution to the audiences' sense of delight. Often invisible, the work engineers do means people enjoy not only beautiful art forms, but the wider environment and building itself.

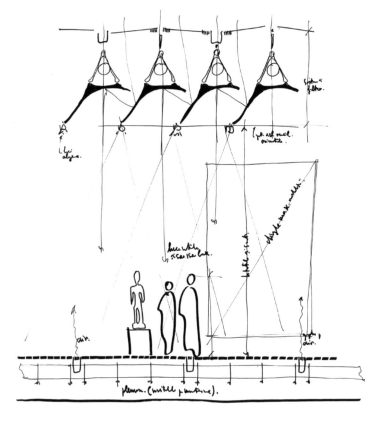

How do you display art treasures in natural light without damaging them?

When philanthropist Dominique de Menil decided to open a museum housing her private art collections, her main request was for daylight. She wanted the art lit naturally. This way, visitors to the Houston galleries could be more attuned to the subtle variations in the works according to time, weather and season.

We worked with the architect Renzo Piano to develop a louvre-style roof made of 300 'light leaves'. These acted as both light filter and heat shield to protect the art. To keep the ceilings free of mechanical services and allow uniform daylight into the galleries, we developed a system to supply conditioned outdoor air at floor level. Completed in 1987, The Menil Collection demonstrates integrated design. Its shading, lighting,

ventilation services and structures are component parts of the architecture. In 2013, it received the Twenty-five Year Award from the American Institute of Architects for the enduring significance of its design.

We have developed the ideas from Menil at the new Renzo Piano Pavilion at the Kimbell Art Museum in Fort Worth, Texas. Here, the daylight-control system can be manually turned to tailor the light for each show and for the season. These louvres have photovoltaic cells which also generate enough electricity to offset up to 70% of carbon emissions from the gallery space's heating, lighting and air systems. Twenty-five years on, our modern louvres prove the old adage: the best ideas really do stand the test of time.

Above left: in Renzo Piano's garden, the collaborative team agree the precise design of the faux cement leaves.

Above right: a Piano sketch shows how the leaves work to filter the level of interior light.

Right: a gallery at The Menil Collection, Texas, shows how the leaves allow uniform daylight into the space.

The result of a winning competition entry in 1971 by then unknown architects Renzo Piano and Richard Rogers, with Arup, Centre Pompidou inspired future buildings by redefining open spatial planning inside.

The Pompidou partnership

This inside-out building turned the world of architecture upside down and gave Paris a new icon. It also transformed the way people connect with art.

There are few better examples of engineering design being so central to building form. Pipes and ductwork are reimagined as part of the overall aesthetic, with colour-coded innards decorating the exoskeleton. Blue tubes circulate air, while green pipes carry water. Yellow is for electricity and red shows how people move around via lifts and escalators. By rendering the invisible visible, visitors and passers-by can 'read' the building's components through its architecture.

Placing the structural elements and building services on the outside of the building offered uninterrupted internal galleries and created spaces that can be flexibly reconfigured to suit temporary exhibitions.

The Lloyd's building, London, UK
Completed in 1986, this was designed with Richard Rogers. It was the first post-war building to be Grade I listed. Like Pompidou, it has its services such as staircases, lifts, electrical power cables and water pipes on the outside of the building as a fundamental part of the design.

"I'm very suspicious of the idea that the architect simply does the drawings and then asks the engineers to build it. There's more to architecture than architecture."

From left to right: Peter Rice, Renzo Piano and Richard Rogers, sitting on a cast steel gerberette on one corner of the Centre Pompidou frame, high above central Paris.

Richard Rogers
The art of collaborative design

From private homes to opera houses, we architects work with shelter and space. In that sense, architecture satisfies one of our most fundamental needs: the need for security. But architecture is not just about designing the built environment. It is an exercise in collaboration – and not just with engineers; it can be working with a planner, a landscaper, an economist, even a philosopher. I resolutely believe that architecture is about teamwork; I'm very suspicious of the idea that the architect simply does the drawings and then asks the engineers to build it. Likewise, the concept of 'the idea', where one lone genius takes all the credit! There's more to architecture than architecture. And that's a stance that Arup, and especially Ove, also takes.

Of course, the client is also part of the team. Clients change their minds; building rates and political situations change continuously; multiple factors can affect what you are doing. All these strands must be brought together, and that can't be done in one individual's head. Such a series of overlapping activities requires a multidisciplinary group of experts, all interacting like a game of ping-pong – they hit the ball, you've got to hit it back. Each person in the group will have their own specialist knowledge to contribute to the project and start discussion.

Finding the right collaborative partner is like finding a good friend – there's no objective test, but you know when you've got one. You start to work well, you exchange ideas, you get a feel for one another: you're on the same quest, so trust is important. Before we began work on the Centre Pompidou, Renzo Piano and I had only worked together on a few residential projects. Essentially, we jumped from bicycles to aeroplanes in one go. With Peter Rice, the Arup engineer on the Pompidou, we very quickly began talking the same language and stimulating one another.

Looking back at the Pompidou, I realise that it is a piece of infrastructure, as we conceived piazzas and roads as well as the building. Peter was a wonderful problem-solver, and architecture is all about solving problems. But he could also talk and describe with such poetic ability. Engineers have to have the ability to experiment and feel confident that an experiment will succeed, but Peter was able to describe why in a way that we as architects could understand.

Of course, engineers and architects work together, though the line between them is often blurred. We ride out the ups and downs together. There are plenty of examples of engineering-as-architecture, from Joseph Paxton's work on the Crystal Palace and Kew Gardens' Palm House, to Nicholas Grimshaw's, Norman Foster's and my own work today. Of course, my favourite is Brunelleschi, who was born in Florence.

For me, city planning projects are the ones that give the greatest satisfaction. These jobs are not only large but also highly complex, because they need to include so many different elements: places to love, laugh, cry, gather, and so on. Arup is strong not only in city planning, but also in linking cities to each other: its extremely sophisticated planners are leading the new railway expansion in Britain and it's thanks to them that we have a much better way to get to Paris than before.

As individuals and as a profession, we have social responsibilities beyond the aesthetic. My concern is that architecture – and therefore engineering with it – is becoming more decorative. Of course, buildings are remembered more for their design than for who solved the problems, but as the old adage goes: "Any fool can make it cheaper; it's a question of whether you can make it better."

Arup has stayed true to the post-war liberal vision of social responsibility that Ove set out. At Rogers Stirk Harbour + Partners, our approach overlaps with Arup's. We have a constitution that enshrines our strong social vision, we are owned by a charity and we offer staff a profit share. It is this sense of working for society and not just for profit that pushes us to do better.

Lord Richard Rogers
Rogers Stirk Harbour + Partners

Top: Leadenhall, designed with Rogers Stirk Harbour + Partners, sits in the heart of the City of London.

Above: the interior of Lloyd's of London.

Snape Maltings Concert Hall, Suffolk, UK
Suffolk Youth Orchestra, with conductor Philip Shaw, at Snape Proms 2015.

Right: Arup SoundLab, New York office.

Birthplace of acoustic expertise

It was composer Benjamin Britten's idea to turn a derelict malthouse in Suffolk into a world-class concert venue.

Converting the space into Snape Maltings Concert Hall was a triumph of sensitive design. Don't be deceived by the simple-looking brick room with pitched timber roof; it was carefully designed to deliver excellent acoustics. By removing the cross-walls that formed the original hoppers, and increasing the height of the perimeter structural walls, we created a space comparable in size to the best European concert halls – with a sound to rival any in the world.

This milestone project was born of our collaborative ethos, creative approach and technical excellence. It also sowed the seeds of our acoustic consultancy, which became the first of many specialist groups where the demand for technical excellence to transform the way buildings are made and how they perform challenged us to develop our in-house expertise.

Today, SoundLab is changing the way

acoustics is used in design. It allows us to simulate the sound of any space. SoundLab is an integral part of the design process – our designers can experience what works and what doesn't during the concept and design phases. That way, they can focus from the start on getting the design right.

We have SoundLabs in many offices around the world: precisely calibrated, acoustically neutral studios where clients can experience different soundscapes first-hand. Everyone can hear how different design choices, from the shape of the space to the materials used, will affect the sound quality.

SoundLab takes a human-centric view of design. It 'translates' quantifiable aural information into a format that everyone can experience and understand. So not only is it a great tool for clients, but it benefits the public too. As well as showcasing the acoustic design of indoor spaces, we use it to demonstrate the noise levels of proposed projects, from wind farms to airport runways and high-speed rail lines.

Sound and space in harmony

Excellent acoustics are critical to the design of performing arts spaces, and depending on the use of the space, the desired acoustic goals vary. In the case of opera, many older opera houses are designed to make sung words clear, with a controlled orchestral sound. Modern opera houses tend to be more reverberant, producing a concert-like orchestral sound. Our clients for the Oslo Opera House wanted the ability to have both.

To achieve this, we developed a novel design approach for the auditorium. By using a cross-section that was wider at the top than at the bottom, this created an upper volume that could sustain reverberance. The space could then be tuned by deploying sound-absorbing curtains that improve vocal clarity for more lyrical opera repertoire or when amplified sound is used. Using SoundLab, we were able to compare the sound with other world-class venues and listen from any of the 1,400 seats in the as-yet-unbuilt space. Today, the floating white opera house, with its excellent views across the Oslofjord and exceptional acoustics, has become a new icon for Norwegians.

Sound quality isn't the only factor dictating the

quality of the audience experience. Often, it's the little things that matter. Feeling too hot or cold can ruin a performance. Which is why, when we pioneered an underfloor ventilation system for the Glyndebourne Opera House in 1994, comfort was front of mind.

A grille incorporated into the design of every seat delivers a steady but barely noticeable stream of air which is warmed by the body heat of the person sitting above. As the air warms, it rises to the roof, driving air circulation in the auditorium. This quiet, low-energy AC system is now common in auditoria today.

As engineers, our interventions must help realise the design. Take Osaka's Maritime Museum (page 28). Rising 35m above the water, its gleaming glass dome is impossible to miss. The challenge was to ensure the glass façade didn't give rise to an overheated interior. Our 'lami-metal' glazing kept air conditioning to a minimum using the most unobtrusive method. We inserted a sheet of perforated metal into each laminated glass panel, limiting the amount of sunlight that could come through. On bright days, the 'lami-metal' looks almost opaque, mirroring the blue sky; in dull weather, it becomes clear.

Behind the 'unbuildable' building

As one of the most structurally ambitious spaces we have worked on since the Sydney Opera House, the National Taichung Theater has rewritten the rulebook. Its standout geometries – a double-curved shell and continuous single surface interior – could not have been achieved even a decade ago. State-of-the-art computational tools and innovative construction techniques have made it possible. We introduced the idea of creating a maze of interlocking truss walls and mixing prefabricated forms with in-situ casting to reduce construction costs and accentuate the purity of this radically expressive architectural form. The maze was prefabricated, brought onsite and overlaid with fine mesh. Concrete was then poured between these meshes to flesh out the continuous curved surfaces that blur the distinction between floor, wall and ceiling.

Cutaway left: the coloured lines in the cross-section show the direction of principal stresses in the material. Their colour and length correspond to the magnitude of the stress. From this, engineers can understand the various load paths throughout the building and use this to decide how best to optimise its structure.

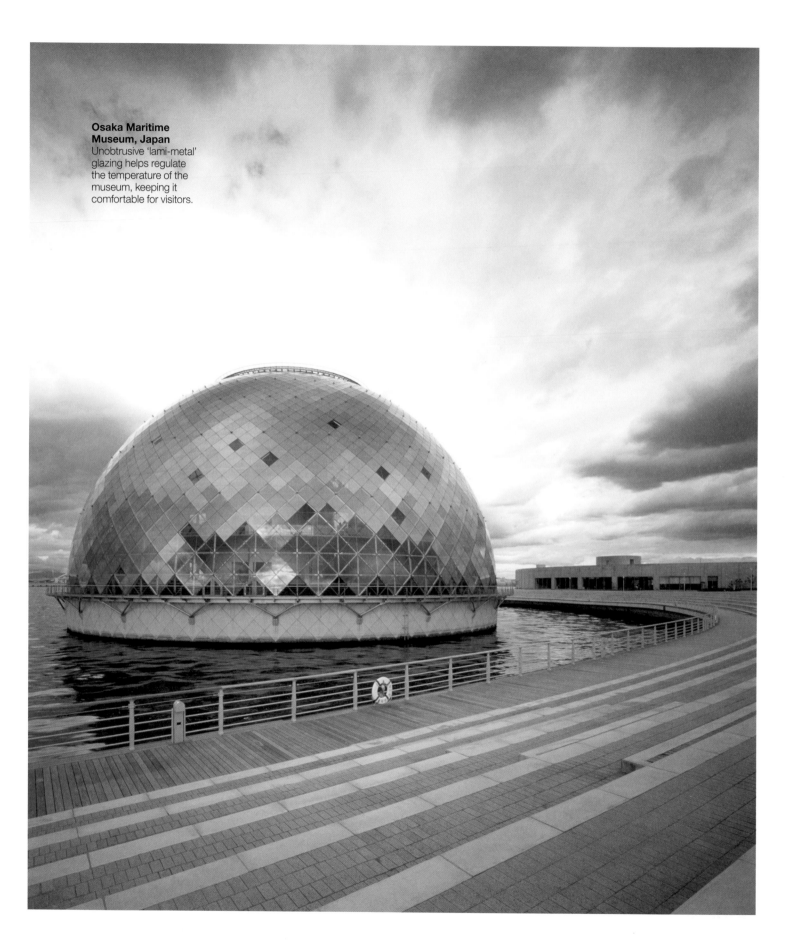

Osaka Maritime Museum, Japan
Unobtrusive 'lami-metal' glazing helps regulate the temperature of the museum, keeping it comfortable for visitors.

Transforming cities

Urban regeneration has come about as the demand for city living has increased. Transport links have been built, entire cities with contemporary facilities and living spaces have sprung up from wastelands, and land has been reclaimed from water to deliver new places to enjoy. To keep pace with this demand, we have combined our specialist expertise, ranging from wayfinding and lobbying to behavioural psychology, with our more established skills such as building and civil engineering. The result is to help bring urban areas to – and back to – life.

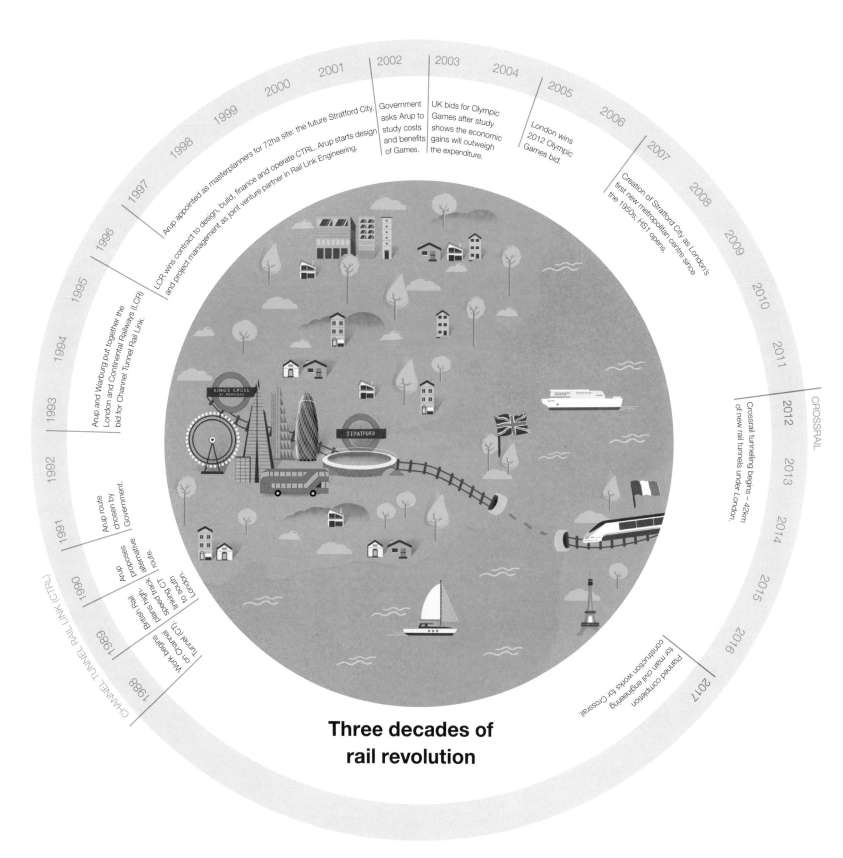

Three decades of rail revolution

1988 Work begins on Channel Tunnel (CT) linking CT in south London.

1989 British Rail plans high-speed track route.

1990 Arup proposes alternative route.

1991 Arup route chosen by Government.

CHANNEL TUNNEL RAIL LINK (CTRL)

1994 Arup and Warburg put together the London and Continental Railways (LCR) bid for Channel Tunnel Rail Link.

1996 LCR wins contract to design, build, finance and operate CTRL. Arup starts design and project management as joint venture partner in Rail Link Engineering.

1997 Arup appointed as masterplanners for 72ha site: the future Stratford City.

2002 Government asks Arup to study costs and benefits of Games.

2003 UK bids for Olympic Games after study shows the economic gains will outweigh the expenditure.

2005 London wins 2012 Olympic Games bid.

2007 Creation of Stratford City as London's first new metropolitan centre since the 1950s; HS1 opens.

CROSSRAIL

Crossrail tunnelling begins – 42km of new rail tunnels under London.

2017 planned completion for main civil engineering construction works for Crossrail.

Stratford: a new city for a new generation

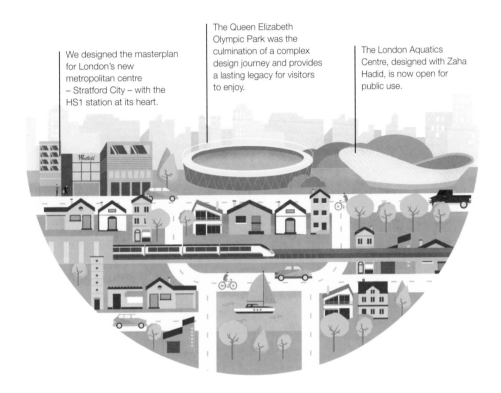

We designed the masterplan for London's new metropolitan centre – Stratford City – with the HS1 station at its heart.

The Queen Elizabeth Olympic Park was the culmination of a complex design journey and provides a lasting legacy for visitors to enjoy.

The London Aquatics Centre, designed with Zaha Hadid, is now open for public use.

Forging a new path

It takes vision to recognise a wider opportunity. In 1989, British Rail announced plans to build a high-speed track connecting London to the continent, with trains departing from Waterloo station, south of the Thames. It got us thinking – could there be a way to make the same connection but with wider benefits?

By then, work had already started on construction of the Channel Tunnel, which links Folkestone in Kent with Coquelles in northern France. However, we were certain there was room for a bolder plan for the route into London that could transform the capital, and the country as a whole.

Out of that thinking came our counterproposal for the Channel Tunnel Rail Link: why not run it into the north of London from the east via Stratford and King's Cross? Not only would it connect the rest of the country with the European rail network, but it could also revive the capital's deprived East End.

Initially, we were a lone voice championing our alternative route, against a tide of naysayers. But we persevered and challenged, analysed and lobbied – and eventually we persuaded.

Today, a once-derelict and inaccessible part of London is changing faster than almost any other area of the UK, with a vibrant, modern metropolitan hub spawning new businesses and nurturing communities. The Channel Tunnel Rail Link, now called High Speed 1 (HS1), has helped bring more than £10bn of regeneration investment into Stratford.

The transformation of the 72 hectares of old rail lands at Stratford by the clever use of the excavated soil from the HS1 tunnels allowed the land to be brought back into use as parkland, and residential and commercial property. Several residential developments, a new shopping core and one station expansion later, Stratford is now unrecognisable from its former self. >

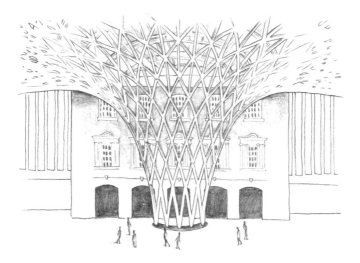

King's Cross, London, UK
Redeveloping the Grade I listed King's Cross station into a transport hub fit for the modern age required clever engineering and sympathetic design. For a decade, our pedestrian modelling team worked to map precisely how many millions of people a year use the station. This detailed insight helped shape the redevelopment. We also pioneered the construction of the diagrid shell structure of the roof, which spans across – and is supported by – perimeter tree columns and a central funnel structure. This design means the new concourse is structurally independent of the historic Western Range building. So the old and the new can sit side by side in complete harmony.

And the 20-year sustainability framework we developed looks set to exceed its initial targets for carbon savings.

The benefits have spread right along the rail line. The new rail infrastructure, linking with London's St Pancras mainline rail station, and the revitalisation of east London were significant factors in winning the 2012 Olympic and Paralympic Games. More importantly, HS1 has reconfigured London's transport landscape. The shift in its centre of gravity to the north and east will have a lasting legacy, both socially and economically.

The line has more than transformed travel between the UK and the rest of Europe – it has transformed London, informing further large-scale tunnelling projects in the city such as Crossrail. And it just goes to show, sometimes it pays to challenge the status quo.

Crossrail, London, UK

As part of HS1, we created the largest tunnels ever formed under London. This knowledge stood us in good stead when it came to Crossrail. Europe's largest civil engineering project will create an east-west high-frequency rail line in London and the South East. Ten new stations are being built, with eight below ground and integrated with the existing London Underground network. The most intensive construction effort involves the two 21km tunnels under the centre of the city.

New land from old

Being on the water served cities well in the past. But as they moved from the industrial into the information age, their waterfronts fell into disrepair and neglect. We are helping cities reclaim their waterfronts and give them back to the people as exciting new parts of the city, creating thriving places to live, work and enjoy.

Transforming formerly no-go areas into vibrant, welcoming places that people can enjoy transforms lives too. Public access to leisure spaces alongside beautiful stretches of water feeds healthy minds and bodies and brings economic and social benefits. The boost from economic regeneration can revive a city's former glories. It can elevate them to a new level, adding value and increasing the tax base in every sense.

Waterfronts are coming full circle, reprising their role as economic and social agents of change.

Transforming the derelict piers along the waterfront into the 5-mile Hudson River Park was an exercise in innovation, collaboration and imagination.

New York can finally make good on that 200-year-old pledge by the City Commissioners: "The rivers will be our parks."

On the waterfront

MANHATTAN, NY

Pier 55

In 2019, the humble pier that was once the landing point for Titanic survivors will become a unique undulating floating park, towering 19m above the Hudson River. Featuring three public event spaces, their acoustics enhanced using our SoundLab technology, we will help bring this one-of-a-kind 'treasure island' to life, setting a new benchmark in defining what a public park can be.

Hudson River Park

Strolling along the rejuvenated Hudson River shoreline, it's easy to conjure up Manhattan's maritime past. After years of neglect, it has been repurposed but its industrial legacy can still be seen in the vestiges of infrastructure lining the shore. As planned, the 550-acre park connects New Yorkers with their heritage at every step. This 5-mile stretch of historic waterfront is the largest new park in New York since the 19th century. Our project management, which involved controlling design standards and managing pedestrian and vehicle movement, helped bring this complex scheme to fruition. The result? Cycleways and sports venues, playgrounds and performance spaces. In essence, fresh air and freedom.

Battery Park City

Amid the towers of lower Manhattan, in Battery Park City, young people can experience the thrill of the great outdoors. Once, it was 92 acres of landfill, but it is now some of the most engaging open space in the city. The property is home to Teardrop Park, a playground inspired by the Catskill Mountains, where we integrated natural materials into the 2-acre site so that children can engage with a more dynamic landscape. Further south, Robert Wagner Jr. Park houses two Arup-engineered pavilions on either side of a statue-oriented axis, with steps cascading down from viewing platforms to form an amphitheatre around the plaza that makes it an ideal location for outdoor events. The park's southern tip caps off with the impressive Pier A, an ambitious restoration project on the oldest pier shed in New York.

East River Esplanade

The city began along the East River, now Manhattan's Financial District. But as it grew, the shoreline became increasingly divorced from city life. Families gave it a wide berth. Now it's all changing. A new mile-long esplanade and cycle path, and an eco-park at Pier 35 have rejuvenated the area. As well as having responsibility for the structural, electrical and geotechnical engineering, we also conducted traffic studies. These enabled us to design better pedestrian access to the park and bikeway. It has become a waterfront park that welcomes all – and marches to the beat of the city once more.

PIER 55

HUDSON RIVER PARK

EAST RIVER ESPLANADE

BATTERY PARK CITY

Creating land out of the sea

The story of the waterfronts of Asia's major cities could hardly be more different from that of the post-industrial West. Far from regenerating derelict land, here it has been about creating much-needed land by reclamation from the sea, with the waterfront an ever-moving boundary.

During the 1970s and 1980s, Hong Kong's growth rate exploded. Over that period, the waterfront of Hong Kong Island moved northwards into the harbour by several hundred metres, in several successive stages, while Kowloon extended westwards.

We have been present in the city for more than 40 years, and it has shaped us as much as we have helped shape it. Hong Kong pioneered a development model with the structure of underground rail stations planned from the outset to support dense commercial and residential development above. We engineered many prominent buildings on the waterfronts of the day, with underground railways beneath the reclaimed land. Many are now inland.

Two of the most recognisable – Two International Finance Centre on the island and the International Commerce Centre on Kowloon – are built in this way, above stations and on reclaimed land.

Above: the Manchester Ship Canal in the 1960s.

Left: today, Salford Quays is a thriving, attractive place to live.

Transforming docks

Truly successful transformations take time and long-term planning. By the 1970s, the formerly thriving docks on the Manchester Ship Canal in England were in disuse and becoming derelict. Starting in the 1980s, we helped Salford City Council begin the area's transformation into Salford Quays with a design of the reclamation and infrastructure works that would kick-start change. The water within the docks was isolated from the polluted canal, and new land routes and bridges linked the 'fingers' of the docks to improve internal connections. Thirty years later, the old docks have been reborn as a cultural destination. Museums and galleries such as the Lowry and Imperial War Museum North have opened and, in 2011, MediaCityUK became the northern home of the BBC. Once a location even the most determined estate agent wouldn't try to sell, it's now a thriving metropolis drawing all to the waterside.

Global urbanisation

It's not just urban regeneration that is transforming the way we live and work. Visionary architectural design, underpinned by inspired feats of engineering, is sending our cities soaring ever skywards. Buildings make a statement about the city. Creating a city with purpose and meaning for people is the holy grail of planning. Across the globe, through innovative design, high-tech engineering and locally influenced masterplanning, we are helping to create liveable, sustainable and thriving cities to meet and exceed the needs of the ever-growing urban population.

**30 St Mary Axe,
London, UK**
Height: 179.8m
Completed: 2004

**Guangzhou International
Finance Center,
Guangzhou, China**
Height: 438.6m
Completed: 2010

**Marina Bay Sands,
Singapore**
Height: 206.9m
Completed: 2010

**Two International
Finance Centre,
Hong Kong, China**
Height: 412m
Completed: 2003

**Canton Tower,
Guangzhou, China**
Height: 600m
Completed: 2010

**China World Tower,
Beijing, China**
Height: 330m
Completed: 2010

Building tall across the decades

Emley Moor Television Tower, West Yorkshire, UK
Height: 329.2m
Completed: 1971

OCBC Bank, Singapore
Height: 197.7m
Completed: 1976

HSBC Main Building, Hong Kong, China
Height: 178.8m
Completed: 1985

Torre de Collserola, Barcelona, Spain
Height: 288m
Completed: 1992

Commerzbank Tower, Frankfurt, Germany
Height: 298m
Completed: 1997

Hillbrow Tower, Johannesburg, South Africa
Height: 270m
Completed: 1971

Hopewell Centre, Hong Kong, China
Height: 216m
Completed: 1980

UOB Plaza 1, Singapore
Height: 280m
Completed: 1992

Central Plaza, Hong Kong, China
Height: 373.9m
Completed: 1992

Taller, safer and more breathtaking

As the technical specialists behind some of the most iconic tall buildings in the world, our thinking has helped owners and architects realise remarkable creations, from towering skyscrapers to statement-making buildings. We have also taken great strides to ensure skyscrapers are safer, leading the way in performance-based design.

If money is no object, building tall is not especially difficult. Doing it in a way that is commercially and operationally efficient is much harder. Massive structural elements, environmental systems and multiple elevator banks all add cost and eat into the total floor space available to generate revenue.

We use sophisticated analysis to make our designs simpler. We fine-tune structures to damp their response to seismic and wind loads, design façades to minimise the load on environmental systems and use intelligent vertical transport systems to minimise the number of elevator banks.

At the heart of what we do is collaboration between client, architect and engineer – simple ingredients that produce better and more breathtaking buildings.

China Central Television (CCTV), Beijing

A spectacular example of structural design: the building's shape looks as if it shouldn't be able to stand up. It took innovation and close collaboration with the architects to link the two leaning towers via a 75m cantilever. We used the entire exoskeleton of the tower to create a stable structure with a diagrid external structural frame. The result is a modern icon. This statement about the future direction of China Central Television also symbolised the start of a new era of construction for Beijing.

Torre BBVA Bancomer, Mexico City, Mexico
Height: 234.9m
Completed: 2015

Raffles City, Hangzhou, China
Height: 250m
Completed: 2016

MahaNakhon, Bangkok, Thailand
Height: 314m
Completed: 2016

China Zun, Beijing, China
Height: 528m
Completion: 2019

Torre Reforma, Mexico City, Mexico
Height: 245m
Completed: 2015

CTF Finance Centre, Guangzhou, China
Height: 530m
Completed: 2016

Goldin Finance 117, Tianjin, China
Height: 596.5m
Completion: 2017

KK100,
Shenzhen, China
Height: 441.8m
Completed: 2011

The Shard,
London, UK
Height: 306m
Completed: 2012

One Central Park,
Sydney, Australia
Height: 117m
Completed: 2013

International
mmerce Centre,
ng Kong, China
Height: 484m
ompleted: 2010

Northeast Asia
Trade Tower,
Incheon, South Korea
Height: 305m
Completed: 2011

CCTV Headquarters,
Beijing, China
Height: 237.5m
Completed: 2012

122 Leadenhall,
London, UK
Height: 224m
Completed: 2014

44

With 24 million citizens, Shanghai is one of the most populous cities in the world. We have frequently worked in China during this period of rapid urbanisation, with the growing scale of projects testament to the country's economic and population growth.

Cities for tomorrow's world

Never before has so much of the world's population lived in cities. Today, 3.5 billion people – and rising – are city dwellers. That's more than half the world's population.

But cities do not arise spontaneously. They are created and grow in response to a complicated set of desires and demands. Born of myriad reasons, from the geographic to the socioeconomic, cities are complex organisms.

We are helping to create liveable, sustainable and prosperous cities that can meet current and future priorities. Our 'integrated urbanism' approach aims to use insights gained from studying the multitude of factors affecting the urban environment.

It is more than just thinking about the large-scale shape of a city. It involves looking at integrated systems such as governance, economics, mobility and telecommunications. It means helping each city identify the priorities and needs appropriate to it, so that we can foster an environment conducive to the characteristics desired in a place. By developing a flexible long-term strategic vision, we can set the foundations for an economically thriving, socially cohesive and culturally appropriate urban environment.

Masterplanning an eco-city

Integration and collaboration are at the core of good masterplanning. One of the best demonstrations of our multidisciplinary approach to masterplanning is Dongtan, situated just outside Shanghai, which – although unbuilt – remains our first eco-city design. The idea of building an eco-city came from conversations at the political level regarding China's rapid urbanisation. We explored how we could shift Dongtan's initial environmental perspective into a widespread ecological approach.

Our proposed masterplan demonstrated how the demands of a rapidly urbanising region could be aligned with sustainability priorities. With a proposed population of 500,000, the compact city – designed so all housing would be within a 7-minute walk of public transport – hoped to be as close as possible to carbon neutral and zero waste. Plans included producing 40% of the development's energy from bioenergy. Naturally ventilated, well-insulated buildings that ran on renewable wind and solar energy would use 66% less energy than a typical building.

The ideas we pioneered have since formed the key parts of many masterplanning projects.

The new city was planned for Chongming Island, the world's largest alluvial island, at the mouth of the Yangtze River. Our plan was to protect and enhance the wetlands by returning agricultural land to a wetland state. These 'rings' of development are clearly seen below.

Rejuvenating cities

In South Africa, we are aiming to rejuvenate a city. Tshwane, the country's administrative capital, is transforming socially and economically. As it sought to overcome its troubled colonial past, ushering in a new spirit of optimism, our challenge lay in understanding and reflecting the changing way in which citizens see themselves. By gaining an insight into the city's changing psyche, we created a strategy that represents people in the city through placemaking. Planned spaces allow informal trading on the streets, while the creation of gathering spaces reflects greater connectivity and accessibility throughout the city. Similar approaches can be seen in other cities.

In Sydney, we are setting the urban framework for its new southern district. We are working to kick-start growth by assessing the opportunities presented by the Central to Eveleigh infrastructure corridor. It consists of the city's busiest railway and transport infrastructure, with access to two major stations and key road networks nearby. Our role includes developing the vision, objectives and principles that underpin the framework, as well as developing the overall transformation and strategy. Stitching the railway line – and the neglected land it lies on – back into the fabric of the city will link diverse communities. It will help an exciting new corner of Sydney to thrive.

Tshwane, formerly known as Pretoria, is being rejuvenated in a way that reflects the spirit of the new South Africa.

A 30-year plan for
the Seychelles

In the Seychelles, we are working closely with the government to
create the first 30-year development plan for the multiple islands that
make up the Seychelles. Setting the vision and direction of growth
for the next three decades meant understanding the overarching
macroeconomic landscape as well as the finer, on-the-ground
detail. The project drew upon a wide range of our expertise, from
economics to spatial planning and ecology. As lead consultants,
we based our team in the Seychelles to better collaborate with a
range of local partners and expert sub-consultants. Working with
local communities was vital for gaining an understanding of the
city's issues, such as the impact of growth upon infrastructure,
resilience, tourism and agriculture. The resulting plan addresses the
pressure on existing roads and other infrastructure in a way that is
environmentally sustainable. It also balances the nation's strategic
needs with local desires, to the cultural and economic benefit of the
whole community.

A new urbanism

The pearl of Singapore, Marina Bay is the culmination of a vision which began four decades ago. With the signature Singapore skyline as a backdrop, Marina Bay is envisioned as a Garden City by the Bay, a 24/7 destination, presenting an exciting array of opportunities for people to explore new living and lifestyle options, exchange news and information for business, and be entertained by rich leisure and cultural experiences in a distinctive environment. Formed on reclaimed land, the development features a number of Arup projects, such as the dynamic Marina Bay waterfront promenade, iconic architectural and engineering marvels such as the Marina Bay Sands, The Helix and Gardens by the Bay. Marina Bay Sands' signature silhouette is of three distinctively shaped hotel towers topped by the spectacular SkyPark, an engineering wonder that is the world's longest public cantilever. We pushed the boundaries to create 3D-modelling techniques that improved our visualisation of the complex technical challenges. At 200m up in the air, straddling three towers, the SkyPark measures 340m from end to end, longer than the Eiffel Tower laid down. With 30 million visitors a year, it is the crowning jewel of a wholly transformative regeneration scheme.

The spectacular SkyPark sits prominently on the Singapore waterfront, with state-of-the-art biodome Gardens by the Bay to the left and the Singapore Flyer on the right.

How a city gets its heart

The Middle East is undergoing dramatic change. We are working in Qatar to redefine how the modern city operates in this region.

In the capital city, Doha, we are the creative force behind the masterplan that will bring Msheireb, a central district in the heart of the city, back to life. This formerly important historic area had lost its vibrancy as well as its prosperity. Our task was to transform it into a destination in its own right, on a par with other global inner cities.

City plans tend to fall into two categories – the large-scale 'civic' masterplan comprising grid patterns, blocks and grand boulevards which we find in New York; and the intricate 'serial' masterplan of Mediterranean cities, comprising pedestrian-scale walkways with interlinked courtyards and numerous small points of interest. What makes Msheireb special is our decision to superimpose the grid and the lattice structures,

and, in doing so, create something that is much more than the sum of the parts. High-quality mixed-use residential developments sit alongside cultural, retail and commercial developments, and the area is well on its way to becoming a civic and social hub.

Total engineering solutions have helped build in sustainability. Large streets are oriented to capture cooling winds blowing in from the Gulf, while the lattice's low-rise buildings provide shade. When finished, Msheireb will have one of the highest concentrations of Leadership in Energy and Environmental Design-certified buildings in the world. In terms of cultural sustainability, we have produced a rulebook for the long-term custodianship of this area. It will help revitalise and protect Msheireb for decades to come and, in doing so, create a legacy of lasting value.

People on the move

Travel is faster and easier than it has ever been.
It is a trend that has been rising over the past decades.
We have been part of that journey, building airports,
rail routes and road links to keep pace with demand.
In airports, our influence is clear across the globe,
from fire safety and seismic design rules, to the
creation of a positive passenger experience through
wayfinding; in rail, we have worked in intercity,
urban rail and freight, ensuring smarter, more
sustainable infrastructure. And in bridge building,
which has the power to transform and link
communities (and countries), we have helped drive
regeneration, employment and investment.

Beijing Capital International Airport, Terminal 3, China
Feats of engineering can combine the human and the aesthetic. The skylights in the soaring roof – 800m at its widest and 3km long – exploit natural heat and light to minimise energy consumption, bathing passengers in gold and red light as they pass through.

Stansted Airport, UK
A pioneer in airport fire safety across the world.

Air travel for a new century

It's not just the destination that counts: it's the journey. Our role in airport design has been to improve the passenger experience – often in invisible ways. At Stansted Airport in the UK, we turned convention on its head to introduce a pioneering fire safety system that worked with the building design. The big glass box structure banished mechanical and electrical services beneath the concourse, while the structural 'trees' that supported the 15m-high lightweight steel roof also carried the services delivering air, light and power.

This design meant we couldn't put in place traditional fire-safety features such as partitioning the space and siting sprinklers and vents in the roof. Our innovative fire-safety strategy used the double height of the terminal as a reservoir for smoke to gather above the heads of the occupants. In extreme conditions, the air conditioning can be reversed to suck the smoke down and out through the trees, giving people extra time to evacuate. >

Around the world in hundreds of ways:
the connections that influence airport design

STN
LONDON STANSTED

HKG
HONG KONG INTERNATIONAL

CONNECTION
FIRE SAFETY

1991
Stansted started to
influence fire safety.

SAW
SABIHA GÖKÇEN
INTERNATIONAL

KIX
KANSAI INTERNATIONAL

CONNECTION
SEISMIC ACTIVITY

8.0
The maximum size of earthquake
on the Richter scale that Sabiha
Gökçen can withstand.

PKG
BEIJING CAPITAL
INTERNATIONAL

LHR
LONDON HEATHROW

CONNECTION
PASSENGER EXPERIENCE

800
Passengers per day ferried by
driverless pods to Heathrow T5.

The safety principles of Stansted have been inspiring a new direction for airport terminal design since 1991. Japan's Kansai International Airport adopts a very similar fire-safety strategy. In addition, the unusual shape of the airport's roof, coupled with the threat of tremors and Japan's seismic design rules – the most severe in the world – called for extensive dynamic analyses. Just four months after opening, the airport passed a real-life test in the form of the devastating 1995 Kobe earthquake.

From Kansai to Sabiha Gökçen International Airport in Turkey, we are well versed in building airports to withstand seismic activity. Istanbul's second international airport sits just 20km from the North Anatolian Fault in one of the most seismically active regions on Earth. When it was built in 2009, it was the largest-footprint building in the world to incorporate seismic isolation. Our design uses 300 isolators to reduce lateral earthquake loads by 80%, enabling the terminal to

JFK
JOHN F KENNEDY
INTERNATIONAL

DXB
DUBAI INTERNATIONAL

CONNECTION
OPERATIONAL READINESS

60+
Trials to ready Dubai
Terminal 3 for passengers.

AKL
AUCKLAND
INTERNATIONAL

MEX
MEXICO CITY INTERNATIONAL

CONNECTION
MASTERPLANNING

120 million
The ultimate planned
capacity per annum of
Mexico City's new airport.

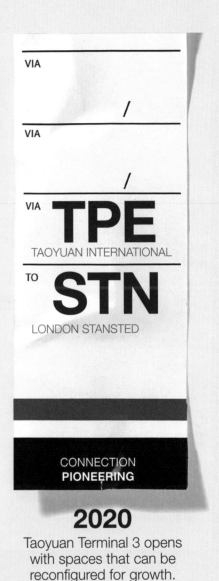

VIA

VIA

VIA TPE
TAOYUAN INTERNATIONAL

TO STN
LONDON STANSTED

CONNECTION
PIONEERING

2020
Taoyuan Terminal 3 opens
with spaces that can be
reconfigured for growth.

withstand earthquakes of up to 8.0 on the Richter scale.

At New York's JFK Airport, tighter airport security hit travellers hard after 9/11. To prevent bottlenecks at check-in and at screening for the JetBlue terminal, we designed the largest multi-gate security checkpoint in the US. We also expanded the international arrivals hall to give JetBlue one of the most convenient and customer-friendly terminals at JFK, built to the new customs standards.

Back in the UK, we helped British Airways transform air travel for its millions of passengers with our vision for Heathrow Terminal 5. As part of the infrastructure we designed, battery-powered driverless pods ferry up to 800 passengers a day from the perimeter car park. They have replaced a fleet of shuttle buses, reducing emissions and giving passengers a stress-free start to their travels. Inside the terminal, departure and arrivals areas, commercial spaces and passenger lounges are flexible >

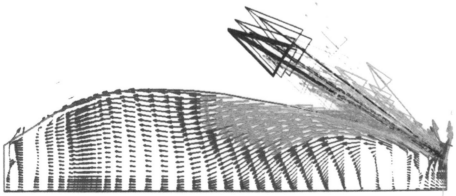

Kansai International Airport, Japan
Kansai's distinctive architecture is informed by integrating structural and mechanical engineering principles with architectural expression. The pioneering use of computational fluid dynamics in the early 1990s (as seen here) enabled us to tune the asymmetrically curved roof, formed by 3-dimensional trusses, to direct high-velocity air jets blowing from one side of the terminal across the entire 80m clear span. The result is an expressive, unobstructed space with a draught-free climate for the main passenger areas.

and can all be dismantled and reconfigured.

We don't just build or remodel airports. We also prepare them fully for operation, ensuring a smooth ride for passengers and airlines from day one. Dubai's Terminal 3, the home of Emirates Airlines, is the largest in the world. To get it ready, we ran more than 60 trials over six months, using 3,500 public volunteers.

Stansted is not the only pioneer. When it opens in 2020, Taiwan Taoyuan International Airport Terminal 3 will set the standard for airport design that absorbs future growth without compromising the original vision. Spaces can be easily reconfigured to accommodate the changing needs of the airport and even the ceiling height can be adjusted to create a more intimate, personal space for passengers. The new terminal will take the art of airport engineering soaring to new heights.

The JetBlue terminal at JFK Airport in New York where our multi-gate design has eased passenger flow through security checkpoints.

The art of motion

Go with the flow. It's the key to an easy life – and it's never so true as when designing transport infrastructure. Our MassMotion pedestrian simulation software helps us to understand crowd movement. Originally developed to help design the Fulton Center transit hub in New York, it helps designers communicate complex problems in a highly visual manner. We can simulate an infinite number of scenarios in an as-yet-unbuilt environment. For stations and airports, we can then build the best passenger experience – and safety – into the design.

MassMotion also reveals how travel can be made faster and easier in existing infrastructure. In Toronto, the software showed how passenger congestion at the city's busiest subway station could be reduced by as much as 63% by adjusting train arrival patterns. At JFK Airport, it helped JetBlue win approval for its terminal by demonstrating that its design allowed passengers to move smoothly around the proposed hub.

Used to model the movement of crowds in everything from hospitals to sports stadiums, MassMotion is the most advanced pedestrian simulation and crowd analysis tool available to the industry.

Moving people around the metropolis

Threading new underground railways beneath densely built cities demands world-class geotechnical and structural engineering. Having established a reputation in Hong Kong for designing high-rise buildings with deep basements and foundations, we were well placed to help the Mass Transit Railway (MTR) Corporation with its massive expansion of the metro network throughout the territory.

Our work began in the 1970s, with the design of deep stations squeezed between existing buildings and, elsewhere, forests of residential towers built above MTR depots. By the 1980s, we were designing deep stations and high-rise buildings directly above them. This trend has culminated more recently in two of Hong Kong's tallest buildings rising 88 and 118 storeys above the major underground MTR interchanges at Central Station and Kowloon Station.

From its origins in Hong Kong, our metro design work has expanded around the world to include Singapore, Taipei, Bangkok, Kuala Lumpur, New York, Toronto, Istanbul, Copenhagen and Riyadh.

It's not just metro systems that we are involved in. Heavy and light-rail systems also play a part in moving people through cities. West Rail for the Kowloon-Canton Railway Corporation in Hong Kong and Crossrail in London (see page 32) transform journey times for huge numbers of travellers.

Light-rail transit (LRT) is more cost-effective for cities with a wider spread and lower population densities. We have designed LRTs in Hong Kong, Kuala Lumpur, the UK and Australia. In Queensland, we have helped to transform the Gold Coast's urban corridor through the construction of a 13km light-rail system. The work included remodelling more than 50 intersections along the route, achieving world-leading reduced wait times.

At its most fundamental, urban rail is integral to the smooth running of the cities and regions. From helping commuters get to work punctually and quickly, to allowing visitors ease of movement around unfamiliar places, an extensive rail network plays a significant part in the wellbeing of citizens.

On such projects, engineering design is a key part of our integrated Total Design approach, but we go beyond this to take into account the greater economic, environmental and social impact. Working together with clients and partners, we are able to offer a service over the entire project life cycle, from conception through to construction, delivery and beyond. And with that expertise, we are helping to cement urban rail's place as the modern city's transportation of choice.

Revolutionising the subway experience

The New York City Subway is the busiest subway system in the western world, carrying more than 1.75 billion passengers a year. Built in the early 20th century, its primary shallow cut-and-cover station design, with no concourses, means that changing travel direction at a station requires passengers to go up to street level to transfer to another platform.

The 16-station Second Avenue Subway avoids all that. Using knowledge from our work in Hong Kong, we are greatly improving the passenger experience. We are providing full design and engineering services to New York's first new line in 80 years. It will transform the passenger experience for millions. By 2020, it will extend more than eight miles on Manhattan's East Side, from Harlem to the Financial District. This will reduce overcrowding on the Lexington Avenue Line, the busiest rapid transit line in the country. Moreover, improved transportation to Manhattan's East Side will stimulate job creation and bring shorter commuting times that will benefit the city for many more years to come.

Creating Europe's longest road-and-rail bridge

When the Øresund Bridge opened in 2000, it cut down the journey time between Malmö in Sweden and Copenhagen in Denmark from an hour-long ferry ride to a 35-minute city-to-city drive.

Part rail-and-road bridge, part underwater tunnel – both Europe's longest at 8km and 4km respectively – and part artificial island, it scythes across the water in a feat of engineering and design. Its gentle curve means the horizon continuously moves across drivers' line of sight, providing sweeping views across the Øresund strait.

We led a design consortium to devise the concept and reference design of the bridge: a 2-lane motorway on the upper deck with two train tracks beneath. Huge sections of the superstructure were prefabricated offsite before being lifted into place by floating cranes. Now 16,000 people start and end their daily – and much shorter – commutes with a glorious panorama.

Above: a cross-section of the bridge. Train tracks lie beneath a 2-lane motorway on the upper deck.

Connecting remote communities

Taking the scenic route is one of life's pleasures. But even the most meandering wanderer might consider 110 miles a detour too far. By crossing Loch a' Chàirn Bhàin, Kylesku Bridge connects communities in the most remote areas of north-west Scotland.

Conventional wisdom in the 1970s was that bridges were straight. However, we believed the deep sea-loch crossing should reflect the contours of its dramatic Highland home. This reflection came by curving the bridge high above the water level while also avoiding making deep cuts into the Hebridean landscape. Its concrete hollow box girder design also needs minimal maintenance, handy in this isolated, wild-weather spot. Severe winters and high winds made construction a challenge. The bridge's centre span was precast on a temporary jetty before being floated out and lifted into position.

By replacing a daylight-only ferry service, Kylesku Bridge has transformed lives in the area. Now, night or day, crossing the loch is as straightforward as a curved bridge can allow.

The watershed wobble

When soldiers march across a bridge, they deliberately break step. They know stepping in unison risks creating dangerous vertical vibrations that could ultimately collapse the structure.

But as hordes of ordinary people started using London's new Millennium Bridge, a phenomenon was brought to light – what's now known as synchronous lateral excitation. As hundreds of pairs of feet walked across, the bridge began to sway sideways and pedestrians unconsciously changed the way they walked to fall in tune with that motion. This set up a synchronised lateral force that exacerbated the initial movement. Multiply this effect by 2,000 pedestrians at a time and the gentle sway became a more uncomfortable wobble. The greater the wobble, the more people walked in step, and the worse it became.

Through exhaustive theoretical and onsite testing, we determined exactly how this previously unknown phenomenon had arisen. Dynamic analysis was used to build a model of the bridge's structure and calculate how it would respond to the synchronising crowd. Once we fully understood what was causing this unanticipated effect, we calculated how to stop it. Ninety-one dampers were installed to effectively absorb more energy than pedestrians on the 320m bridge are able to produce. Our discovery and eventual solution have changed bridge-building worldwide as we published our results for the global bridge-design community to use. And the bridge's unhappy wobble? It's now firmly fixed.

Out of hours: leisure, learning and art

Never before have so many people had access to sport, learning, science and culture. Whether they want to attend an event or watch it at home, benefit from a new scientific discovery or enjoy outdoor art, our environment is richer than ever before. As trusted advisers, capable of delivering outstanding results, we are helping create host cities for major sporting and exhibition events that will go on to have long-term social and economic benefits. The stimulating environments for places of learning, research and scientific discovery that we are developing are leading to new discoveries that will benefit many. And through our collaborations with artists, we are ensuring that art, previously the preserve of a privileged few, is accessible for all.

Sport home reinvented

Sporting events such as the Olympic Games and the FIFA World Cup have global appeal. Host cities are keen to capitalise on the economic and political boost they can bring. They create a lasting impression for locals, visitors and viewers at home – and stadiums are often the stages upon which this aim plays out.

The best are great for athletes, fans and the host city itself. For us, venue-building has flexibility at its core. Stadiums need many lives beyond that first role, from adaptable modes that allow different sports to be played in one venue to a complete change of use that enables them to integrate into the local community long after the last fan has gone home.

The National Aquatics Center, 'Water Cube', Beijing, China
The design of the former Olympic swimming venue, now a water park, is inspired by the formation of soap bubbles. It has a self-cleaning façade made from a translucent plastic 100 times lighter than glass and much better at collecting heat, saving on both lighting and heating. This material also allows for much better acoustics. Around 20% of heating comes from solar energy, while 80% of rain and wastewater are recycled and used for the pools, further reducing the building's impact on precious resources.

Purpose-built for every sport

Singapore Sports Hub is the first stadium in the world to be purpose-built for football, rugby, cricket and athletics, as well as concerts and festivals. A moveable tier of seats can be pushed forward when the track is not in use, so there's no compromise of the spectator experience, whatever the event.

We worked on all architectural and engineering aspects of the project, from urban design and architecture to blast engineering and lighting. The retractable ultra-lightweight dome roof – designed in just five months with more than 100km of steel tubular sections, 26,000 elements and 40,000 welded connections – provides shade during events but allows natural daylight to reach the pitch at other times. When operational, air is delivered to every seat via a carbon-neutral cooling system.

The Sports Hub has formed an integral part of the Marina Bay masterplan to reposition Singapore as a great place to work, live and play. Its versatility means everyone from yoga devotees to cyclists uses it, allowing the Sports Hub to become a true beacon of wellbeing for the city.

A stadium with no compromises

The beautiful game has few homes as passionate as the city of Manchester. Our brief was to design an athletics stadium for the 2002 Commonwealth Games that could afterwards be converted into a world-class home for Manchester City Football Club. The conversion took just 12 months from the day after the closing ceremony: an astonishing feat.

A dual-use stadium, where a running track encircles a football pitch, severely compromises the experience for football spectators. It puts them too far from the action. In our design, the athletics field was lowered several metres by excavating the soil and installing a new lower tier of seating around the perimeter. This automatically put spectators closer to the pitch.

Through careful planning, the City of Manchester stadium has come to symbolise the ongoing transformation of one of the city's poorest boroughs. The reviving fortunes of the club and increasing numbers of non-game day visitors have helped attract private sector investment which, in turn, has created jobs, homes and community facilities. By making sport and leisure facilities accessible to locals, it continues to build a legacy everyone can be proud of.

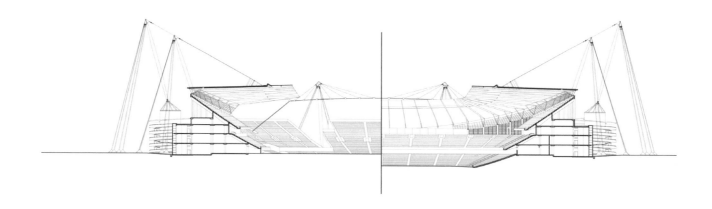

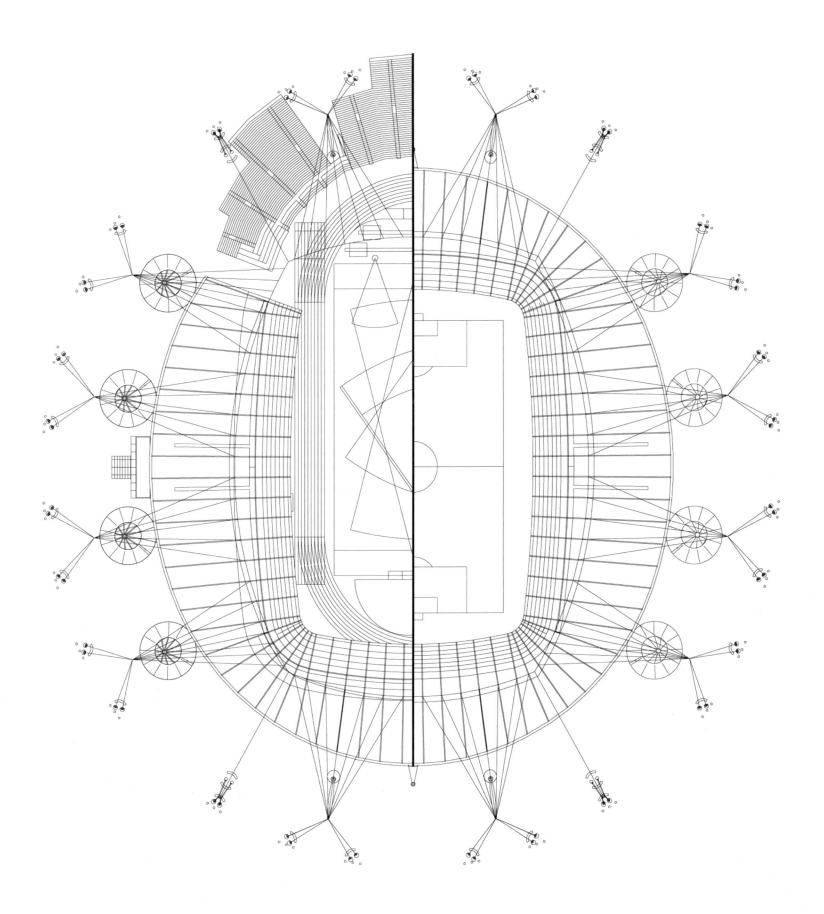

79

Legacy in action

The London Aquatics Centre is a people's arena designed primarily with legacy in mind. The 17,500-seat Olympic swimming and diving venue needed to be converted into a facility that could host international competitions, as well as serve the local community. We designed temporary stands (known as the 'wings') to accommodate extra seating for the Games, readily adapted to the iconic architecture that forms part of its legacy.

Designed to invoke the fluidity of water in motion, the wave-like roof is testament to how effectively our specialists worked with the architect. Its complex geometry and integrated technology required the extensive use of 3D modelling, with models being shared across different professions and industries, making the most of our

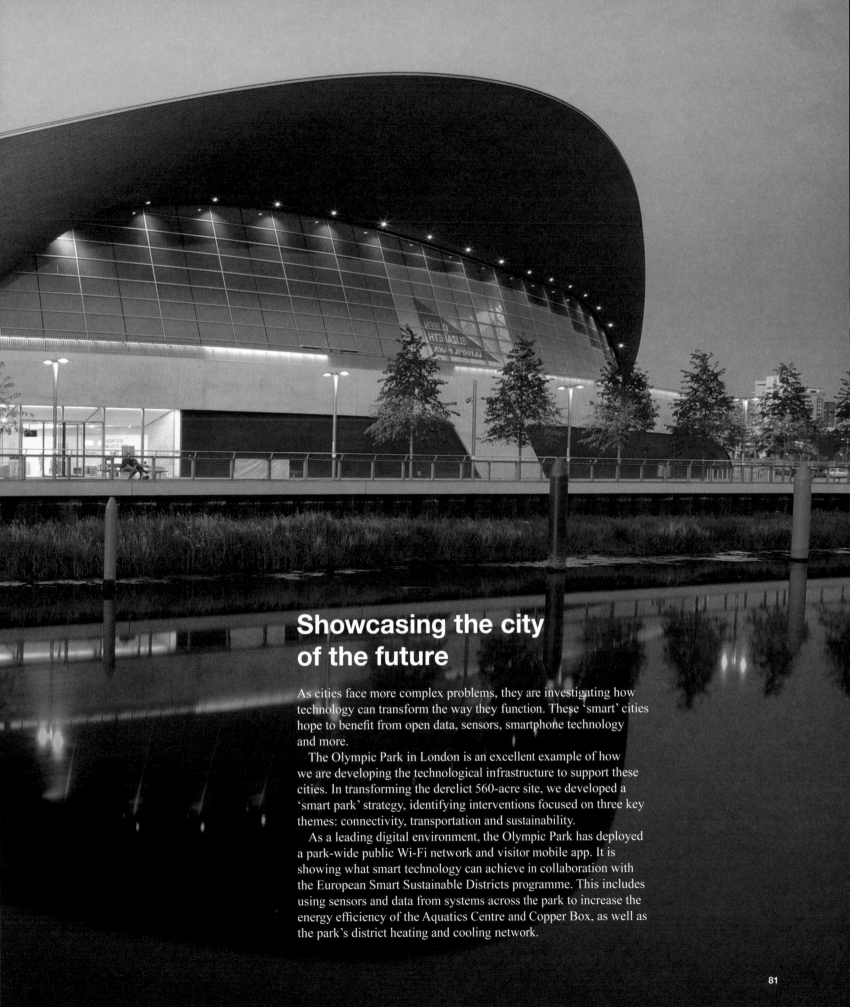

Showcasing the city of the future

As cities face more complex problems, they are investigating how technology can transform the way they function. These 'smart' cities hope to benefit from open data, sensors, smartphone technology and more.

The Olympic Park in London is an excellent example of how we are developing the technological infrastructure to support these cities. In transforming the derelict 560-acre site, we developed a 'smart park' strategy, identifying interventions focused on three key themes: connectivity, transportation and sustainability.

As a leading digital environment, the Olympic Park has deployed a park-wide public Wi-Fi network and visitor mobile app. It is showing what smart technology can achieve in collaboration with the European Smart Sustainable Districts programme. This includes using sensors and data from systems across the park to increase the energy efficiency of the Aquatics Centre and Copper Box, as well as the park's district heating and cooling network.

Putting passion
into learning

As it is with stadiums, so it is for places of learning and
scientific discovery – stimulating environments generate
spectacular results. By creating exceptional research
environments for universities and institutes around the
world, we are helping to inspire the greatest minds in
science. The aim is synonymous with Total Design:
collaborations that yield world-changing answers to the
challenges facing us.

**Sir Thomas White building,
St John's College, Oxford, UK**
With white pre-cast concrete
exoskeletons linked in an L shape,
this 1970s building reinterpreted the
traditional Oxbridge quad. Modern
complex building functions require
us to rethink building techniques
and materials. The expressive use of
engineering systems is a distinguishing
feature of 20th century architecture.

A living lesson in environmental science

The California Academy of Sciences is at the forefront of environmental science, so it was no surprise that it called on our design team to deliver one of the most environmentally friendly museums in the world. A wealth of energy-saving innovations are incorporated into the structure to keep its carbon footprint award-winningly low.

Sustainability was behind every element of this design. Openings in the dome-like roof allow breezes from the Pacific Ocean to ventilate the exhibition hall. Two-thirds of its insulation comes from recycled denim, courtesy of the nearby Levi jeans factory. Solar energy provides power and sea water cools spaces. It is the largest building in the world to receive a Platinum rating for Leadership in Energy and Environmental Design.

Transparent glass walls and a 2.5-acre living roof help it blend into its park setting. The building appears as if a piece of Golden Gate Park has been lifted up and the museum slid underneath. It is the physical manifestation of the Academy's mission – to explore, explain and protect the natural world.

Harnessing the light fantastic

How do you lure the world's best plant scientists to your university? By building a world-leading research facility.

Sustainability and adaptability are the hallmarks of Cambridge University's Sainsbury Laboratory. The way daylight illuminates the laboratories sets them apart from other facilities.

Natural light floods the workspaces via glazed skylights set upon 3m-deep light funnels. This prevents glare while allowing daylight in, and creates an inspiring environment for scientific research.

The Botanic Garden was founded by John Stevens Henslow, Charles Darwin's tutor, in the 1830s. The University Herbarium, which contains specimens brought back by Darwin from the Beagle voyage, is located in the heart of the Sainsbury Laboratory.

The laboratory's design takes account of future changes in scientific practice, while remaining true to its Grade II listed setting.

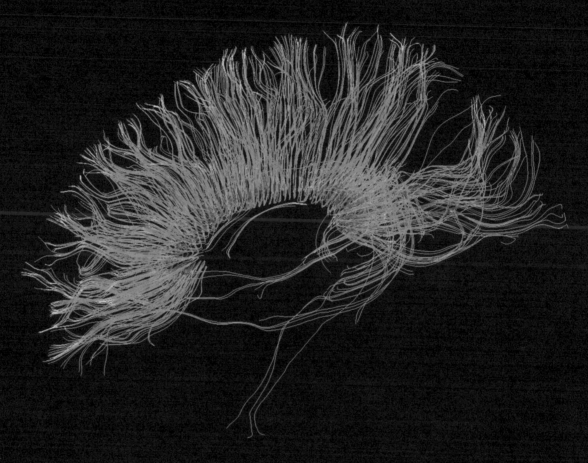

Helping to solve the mysteries of the brain

Understanding how brains process information is one of neuroscience's greatest challenges. The new Sainsbury Wellcome Centre brings together world-leading experimental and theoretical neuroscientists to solve the mystery.

The centre at University College London provides an unparalleled environment for state-of-the-art research into neural circuits and behaviour. To develop a low-carbon laboratory, we used demand control ventilation, a UK first. Sensors determine the level of contaminants in the exhaust air, and the ventilation is adjusted accordingly. We optimised vibration performance to allow delicate scientific work, and engineered double-height laboratories to allow for large experimental rigs. So now the best minds can study the inner workings of the brain with the best possible tools.

Winning formula for lab design

Princeton University is attracting leading chemists with a state-of-the-art facility. The Frick Chemistry Laboratory achieves 30% energy savings with a highly insulated façade, chilled-beam cooling, a heat recovery system and one of the largest integrated photovoltaic arrays in the US.

The building also reinterprets the typical lab layout. Connecting everyone via a soaring 23m glass atrium, it inspires and encourages collaboration. Minds are brought together over coffee as well as the workbench. Forging new bonds — just the way to create chemistry.

A new approach to beating disease

Could this be the place where scientists find the cure for cancer? The Francis Crick Institute in London is a new type of biomedical research facility bringing together experts from six of the UK's most successful scientific and academic organisations. The building embodies the collaborative aspect of Total Design. It has been designed to foster collaboration across different scientific disciplines and speed the transition from breakthrough to treatment.

We created a full-size lab mock-up so scientists could have real input into the design. The result is a complex with shared facilities and open-plan layouts. London's new science hub will attract international talent and be the home of discoveries that will shape a better world.

Art, but not as you know it

Creativity is deeply embedded within our DNA. Our designers enjoy straddling the boundaries between engineering, design and creativity, often collaborating with the artistic community. We have worked with a broad range of artists, from musicians such as Lou Reed to sculptors such as Anish Kapoor and Antony Gormley, designers such as Thomas Heatherwick and artists such as Janet Echelman.

When Janet Echelman conceived a diaphanous net-like sculpture to float above the Gates Foundation HQ in Seattle (pictured), our role was to devise its geometry and means of fabrication and design. We had never before worked with sculpture that used rope or twine. Our willingness to experiment and explore new methods meant that we turned to the language of scripts and algorithms to understand how these forms behaved. We then translated the sculpture's complex 3D blueprint into a 2D knitting pattern. Using highly customised wireless controls, the sculpture now acts as a canvas for unique lighting projections, known as 'Sunrise Scenes'.

It was the first of many Arup collaborations with Echelman, and her artworks have gone on to grace other cities, including London's Oxford Circus, with their light and form. The myriad knots and connections of these ever-changing sculptures have a social value. They serve as an inspirational reminder of how a single person can affect countless lives.

**Angel of the North,
near Gateshead, UK**
Curved steel contours and a wingspan
approaching jumbo-jet proportions
have helped the Angel of the North
achieve iconic status. With its design
also reminiscent of a mine shaft,
Antony Gormley's creation celebrates
Britain's industrial past while embracing
the modern age. We resurrected local
shipbuilding skills and combined them
with boundary-pushing 3D modelling
technology to bring the sculpture to life.

UP, and away!
Sculpting with light is one of our most prominent influences on the built environment. In 2012, our 'UP, and away!' installation for the Vivid Sydney and Luminance! Singapore festivals unleashed childhood dreams of flying free. It connected psychedelic light-up wings to recycled bicycles via an intelligent circuit board. The installation has toured the world, including London and Shanghai.

94

Order from chaos

Climate change, population growth, rising inequality, depletion of resources, natural disasters. The list of challenges the world faces is long, and growing. Our integrated methodology and flexible approach enable us to play a significant role in helping cities tackle these challenges. Building a more sustainable world is not just about preserving the Earth's finite resources. It is also about giving our cities the ability to be resilient; seeking incremental as well as revolutionary change from global industries; and building in the flexibility to allow our systems to cope with a rapidly changing world.

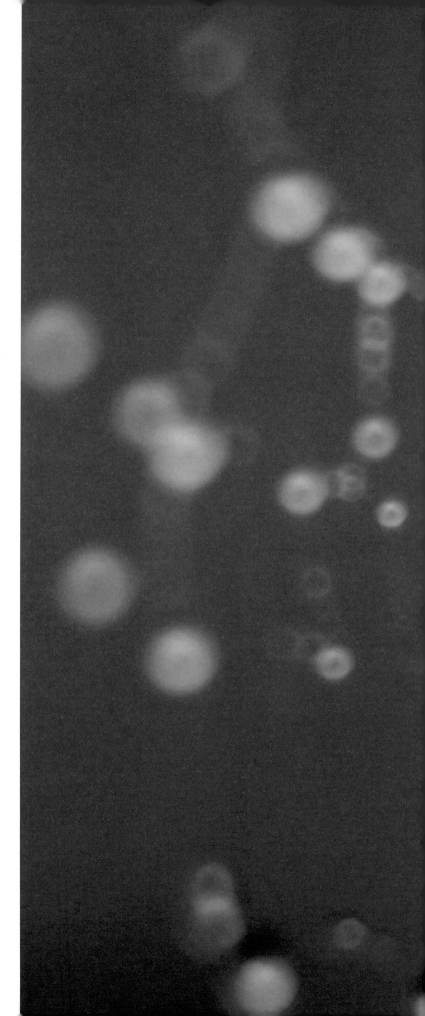

A climate for change

Tackling climate change is a complex systemic issue. From rainwater harvesting at one end of the spectrum to rising sea levels at the other, it needs the collaboration of governments, cities, corporations and society at large to have a real chance of making a difference.

Our partnership with the C40 Cities Climate Leadership Group (C40) is one way we are helping galvanise people into taking collective action. Together, we aim to advance knowledge about the role cities can play in tackling climate change. Over the next three years, we will be working with C40, pouring US$1m into designing solutions for climate action.

Our hope? That by measuring key data we can help cities identify opportunities faster to make significant inroads into reducing greenhouse gas emissions, from clean energy programmes to lower-carbon transport solutions.

C40 represents more than 600 million people across more than 80 cities – that's a quarter of the global economy. By sharing best practice and promoting sustainability, adaptability and resilience across this network, we will be one step closer to minimising the effects of climate change.

Connecting the world: the C40 Cities Climate Leadership Group is about collective action. *The Climate Action in Megacities 2.0* research report that we carried out for the C40 in 2014 recorded 8,068 climate actions taken by C40 cities, almost double that recorded in 2011. The report proves that what happens in C40 cities matters to the whole world.

Arup has provided technical and strategic support to many organisations, including the World Bank, INGOs and NGOs, following the Nepal earthquake in 2015.

Opposite: building construction in the aftermath of the 2005 Pakistan earthquake using the 'dhajji dewari' building technique.

Rising from disaster

We have been contributing to disaster response, helping communities to rebuild their lives, both in the immediate aftermath and longer term, for more than 30 years.

During the 2005 earthquake in Pakistan, thousands were killed by the collapse of poorly designed and constructed buildings. Through advanced structural analysis, we strengthened the case for using a centuries-old local construction technique to build affordable, seismically resistant housing. Advanced structural analysis software showed how 'dhajji dewari' construction (a timber frame with stone and mud mortar infill) could enable people to rebuild cheaper, more resilient, sustainable homes.

In 2012, after Hurricane Sandy hit New York, we worked with the city to identify key issues and propose solutions for housing in flood-prone areas. This was used by the city to help residents rebuild their homes in a more resilient way.

In New Zealand, we supported the emergency response to the devastating Christchurch earthquake of 2011. This helped minimise further damage and loss of life. It also improved understanding of seismic hazards so that new buildings would be better able to withstand them.

Successful disaster management is also about returning an affected area to normality as quickly as possible. As a member of the Global Earthquake Model Foundation, we are helping to raise awareness about earthquake risk and how best to manage this through methods such as financially incentivising seismically resilient construction. Our Resilience-based Earthquake Design Initiative (REDi) Rating System describes planning and design criteria for the next generation of buildings to better withstand and recover from future earthquakes and flooding disasters. We piloted the REDi framework on the 181 Fremont Tower in San Francisco, which is on its way to achieving a REDi Gold rating.

By speeding up the rate at which infrastructure is rebuilt following a disaster, we, in turn, help people rebuild their lives.

Keeping the water flowing

Water is the essence of life – and of cities. In Adelaide, severe droughts and the anticipated effect of global warming made developing a climate-independent water supply critical. Having the largest desalination plant in south Australia means the city no longer relies on rainfall for its drinking water. We designed a 12km pipeline, running through residential and sensitive environmental areas, which connects the plant with the existing water supply network. Adelaide can now meet 50% of its annual water requirements.

In Asia's fast-growing and congested cities, it is often constructing new infrastructure that is the biggest challenge. The Yannawa district of Bangkok lacked any system for collecting sewage. Waste simply made its way into the network of 'khlongs', turning these canals into open sewers. In gridlocked Bangkok, the city's aim to build a sewer collection and treatment system without causing traffic chaos seemed impossible. We came up with a solution to the logistical nightmare that had defeated previous attempts.

Using the established technique of pipe-jacking, but scaling it up, we laid 55km of major sewers beneath the canals, dramatically minimising disruption to the roads. With little land available to build the wastewater treatment plant, our adoption of an innovative treatment system enabled us to design a multi-storey plant on a much-reduced footprint.

In 2000, Yannawa was the first major environmental project to become operational in the Thai capital and remains one of our most significant urban water engineering projects. Now two million people can benefit from reliable wastewater collection, and the canals are much cleaner.

Lake Mead, Nevada, US
At 180km long, this is the largest man-made reservoir in the US, with the water contained by the Hoover Dam. Drought has posed a serious threat to supply, causing water levels to fall by more than 30m since 2000. It is now less than half full. The two intake shafts drawing water from the lake would be inoperable if the levels continued to drop. We developed a deep-water intake on the lakebed – Intake 3 – 100m below the surface. In one of the most complex tunnelling operations ever attempted, we designed a 200m-deep shaft and a 5km-long bored tunnel deep below the lake to connect with the new intake. Pulling the 'plug' meant flooding the intake so the water pressure would be approximately equal to the pressure exerted by the lake above. The 8.6 US ton steel bulkhead was then buoyant enough for a crane on a barge to lift it off. This 'Third Straw', as it's known, will help safeguard the water security of this region for many more years.

75MW Kalkbult photovoltaic power plant, Kalkbult, South Africa.

Facing a lower-carbon future

Fossil fuels are responsible for 70% of greenhouse gas emissions. To halt the release of global greenhouse gases and slow down the progression of climate change, we need to wean ourselves off them.

Tackling issues surrounding energy security, affordability and sustainability – the 'Energy Trilemma' – will also be key to finding viable lower-carbon energy alternatives. Solutions such as wind, solar, geothermal, nuclear power, microgrids and district heating all have a part to play in addressing these issues, but focusing solely on one aspect of the trilemma is likely to exacerbate the other problems.

We are encouraging energy efficiency in the built environment and helping organisations take responsibility for this. The Green Engage Online sustainability tool we created for the InterContinental Hotels Group helps hotels identify energy efficiencies and cut costs. It has been rolled out to 4,700 hotels worldwide, saving millions of dollars in energy costs.

Perhaps the greatest part of the challenge is scaling up the use of renewable energy. In South Africa, where constant blackouts threaten economic growth, we have advised on several renewable energy projects. These include the 75MW Kalkbult photovoltaic plant and the Rosherville research facility, which will test nine configurations of photovoltaic panels to inform future installations. Such projects will help cement lower-carbon energy as a viable solution to climate change.

The rigs that can be reused

As global energy demands increase, traditional oil and gas companies are constantly on the lookout for new pastures. The pursuit of these – be it new gas and oil fields or new technologies – can often have high financial and environmental costs. Where possible, we are supporting the oil and gas industry in pursuing its commercial objectives in an economical fashion, while at the same time encouraging it to minimise the environmental impact. Put simply, we want to leave nothing behind on the seabed.

We have pioneered several cost-effective ways to develop oil and gas reserves. In the 1980s, we created a new style of 'lightweight' concrete oil platform: the Concrete Gravity Substructure (CGS). This can be built almost anywhere and can be 25% cheaper than steel. In the late 1990s, we developed the Arup Concept Elevator (ACE) platform: a mobile drilling platform that can be reused in different locations.

At a time when almost all oil platforms were one-offs, designed for a particular site and then scrapped, this quality represented an advance in offshore platform engineering. The platforms can be installed in volatile seas remote from significant marine centres. Examples include the Ravenspurn oilfield out in the North Sea, where we installed the first CGS. The Wandoo Oil platform, located in Australian waters, had to be towed 1,700km through the Indian Ocean. We precisely installed it on the seabed, fitted it with a topside and connected everything with 9km of subsea pipelines. It was truly a triumph of engineering collaboration.

In the case of the Malampaya deep-water gas-to-power project in the Philippines, we extended the life of the first CGS in Asia by installing a second – adjoining – platform: the new ACE structure is a cost-effective and environmentally sensitive solution.

Our first ACE platform was shipped from South Korea to West Natuna Sea in 2001, and raised to its final in-service elevation within 48 hours. Since then, we have developed our ACE platforms for specific niches.

Sometimes, it takes a radical concept to stimulate a whole industry to improve. Such innovations are helping the oil and gas industry adapt to meet today's challenges.

Decarbonising data

As concern for our limited resources grows, we are looking into practical solutions to seemingly intractable problems. The information and communication technology industry is responsible for 2% of total global greenhouse gas emissions. That is on a par with the aviation industry – and the figure is set to double by 2020.

In 2008, we worked with Citigroup to develop a leading environmentally friendly data facility. The Citi Data Centre in Frankfurt uses design innovations such as reverse water osmosis to recover 90% of wastewater, and has cut energy use by 72%. Having more in common with a high-tech workplace than a storage centre, it's providing a better quality of life for employees too.

If every data centre in the world were built like the Citi Data Centre, it would save enough energy to power a country the size of Belgium.

Net zero

At first glance, it's BedZED's unusual architecture that catches your attention – the turfed roofs and colourful 'spouts' emerging from them. But this visionary mixed-use development is special for a very different reason: it is the UK's first and largest carbon-neutral community. When it opened in 2002, BedZED represented a step-change in sustainable building, demonstrating how people can live within the planet's means.

The brownfield housing-and-workspace development in south London pulled together a range of simple-seeming ideas. We provided the energy engineering and demonstrated the viability of using an integrated design process. Every dwelling has a sky garden or terrace and there is onsite sewage treatment and rainwater recycling. A combined heat and power plant runs on biomass, while solar panels generate enough electricity to power 40 electric cars, representing 16% of the development's energy requirements.

The BedZED project is a showcase for how our Total Design approach works in harmony with the goal of sustainability. It stands as a successful experiment in how we can live within our environmental means.

The biocomposite age

Pressure on the planet's natural resources is increasing, driven by the global population explosion and nations' pursuit of economic growth. The UK construction industry alone uses more than 400m tonnes of material each year. It is one of the country's biggest consumers of natural resources by sector. Building sustainability into design at every level remains a key area of development for us.

We are helping to develop construction materials based on renewable materials. Biocomposites are made from a mixture of fibres such as flax (see above), hemp and the natural resins that are the by-products of processing corn, sugar cane and other crops. At the end of their service life, they can be recycled, composted to fertilise new plants or used as carbon-neutral fuel.

As part of the European BioBuild project, we co-created the world's first biocomposite unitised façade panel, designed for use in commercial office buildings. It costs the same as a conventional unit but consumes 50% less energy during production. The parametrically designed lightweight panel also meets stringent thermal, structural and international fire performance requirements.

In collaboration with architects, materials specialists and manufacturers from seven European countries, we proved the viability of biocomposites as alternatives to traditional materials such as aluminium and concrete.

"Total Design is about a united approach, designing a built environment for people so that they can work in a healthy way and interact productively."

Ngaire Woods
A global approach

It might seem unlikely to mention the philosophy of Total Design in the same breath as global organisations such as the World Trade Organization (WTO), the United Nations (UN) and the International Monetary Fund (IMF). But their core purposes are shared. They are focused on bringing people together to deliver on aims that tackle the threats and opportunities of globalisation, whether they concern a better environment, security or economic efficiency. In a world that is rapidly changing, the similarities in purpose will become even more apparent.

Globalisation – an increasing interdependence and flow of ideas, trade, capital and resources across borders – is an accelerating trend. And that means the philosophy of Total Design, which has shaped the work of Arup for decades, stands it in good stead to face current and future challenges.

This trend, in part fuelled by technologies that enable everything to be done faster, is in the main a positive one. Better integration between countries and regions across the world means there are greater opportunities to receive investment, ideas, talented individuals and cheaper goods from other countries.

But, like many world-shaping agendas, there is also a downside to globalisation. If not carefully managed, it can disrupt secure lifestyles, making people vulnerable. The economic crash and subsequent Great Depression during the 1930s came about as a result of a failure to manage the rapid period of globalisation that began at the start of the 20th century. History repeated itself in the 2008 financial crash, which forced people to take notice of the dangers of unregulated flows of finance and capital.

Organisations such as the WTO, the UN and the IMF were set up to consider multiple elements that bind countries and benefit a large number of people. In common with these, Total Design is about a united approach, designing a built environment for people so that they can work in a healthy way and interact

productively. Total Design also takes into account people's safety and security in its solutions. The fear and insecurity that globalisation can perpetuate are both psychological, to do with identity, and physical – it's about having the physical means to live, but it's also about physical security. Total Design can reinforce the identity of the community, creating a safe space and community in which people can interact.

Aside from its people-centric aspect, Total Design also looks at the environment itself, at sustainability and its immediate impact: whether something is polluting, how it's polluting and how we can create a virtuous circle to replenish rather than deplete our environment.

There are similarities between Total Design and good governance. When you're thinking about a building, you're immediately making choices about whether you're building something that needs to last 100 years, or something temporary. Similarly, in global governance, we have to think clearly about the difference between short-term structures for rapid reaction crisis management (such as a Leaders Summit) and long-lasting institutions that make cooperation among countries possible.

Among the coming global challenges and opportunities is the world of digital, artificial intelligence and the internet of things. This will hugely affect Arup's Total Design philosophy, because it means that our physical world becomes linked to human beings in a completely different way; in a way that redefines who human beings are, what they know about each other, and how they interact with each other, their things and their spaces. That's a revolution not just in what buildings can do, but also for human beings, in terms of what their boundaries are and who they are.

Ngaire Woods
Inaugural Dean of the Blavatnik School of Government, University of Oxford and Professor of Global Economic Governance. Non-Executive Director, Arup Group Board.

One world

Increasingly, the world acts as one. We are working across the globe to engineer change that makes a meaningful difference to people's lives. We imagine and implement new solutions to old problems for those in need. In all sectors, but especially those that touch the lives of the underprivileged, the sick and the under-educated, we aspire to create a social impact that extends beyond the visible legacy of the projects we design. With high-tech innovation, such as earthquake-resistant hospitals in California and sustainable healthcare façades in London, we are future-proofing the places people need most.

Connecting communities

Bridges provide vital lifelines. However, in many places, the lack of bridges limits access to healthcare, education and even food and drink. Bridges to Prosperity, a charity that has transformed communities by building footbridges over often impassable rivers, has just completed its 200th bridge.

After working on several of these projects, we collaborated with the charity to develop an open-source software tool (bridgeTOOL) that enables the rapid design of suspension bridges. Working on a pro bono basis, we road-tested the tool in Rwanda and, with the help of the local community, built a 50m suspension bridge that serves a population of 10,000.

Our tool has given local people the knowledge to build simple and locally appropriate footbridges by themselves. The result has empowered rural communities to end their isolation.

Rwandan villagers build the Muregeya bridge with the help of Arup engineers.

UCH Macmillan Cancer Centre, London, UK
At the Cancer Centre, the wellbeing of the patient comes first. Alongside this, our innovative glazing system, with solar panels, green roof and connection to the local district heating network, has helped to reduce carbon emissions by 20%.

112

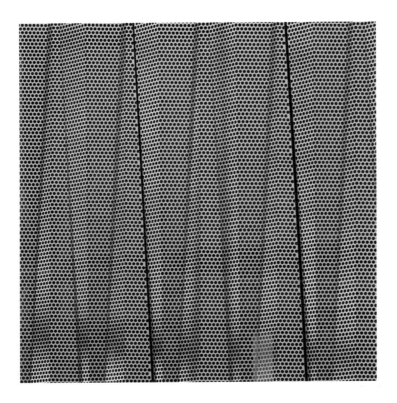

Healthier places,
healthier people

At 148m tall, Guy's Hospital in London is the world's tallest healthcare building. Some 35 years after its tower was built in 1973, it was in need of a facelift. Our retrofit improved energy efficiency and reduced carbon consumption. The 33-storey tower – which would once have been deemed unsalvageable – was reclad using sustainable technologies, such as solar-selective glass to control solar gain in summer and maximise daylight in winter.

Meanwhile, the Manchester Proton Beam Therapy Centre is due to open at the Christie Hospital in 2018. One of our biggest design challenges was the radiation-shielding walls that enclose the proton beam equipment. Embedded in these walls, which are up to 5m thick, is a web of conduits delivering essential electrical, ventilation and plumbing services. Creating the right fit between the specialist equipment and the building wrapped around it was crucial, as was designing a structure highly resistant to vibration and settlement. When complete, the Christie will be the largest single-site cancer centre in Europe.

By helping these buildings come to fruition, we are modernising some of the UK's – and the world's – most renowned hospitals.

Above: we used sustainable technologies to reclad Guy's Hospital, London.

Engineering spaces that heal

Built in the grounds of cancer hospitals, Maggie's Centres empower cancer sufferers to be active participants in their own treatment, providing advice and support to one another along the way. The design ethos is central to this. By providing a calming, reflective space, patients and their families can step out of the hubbub and try to come to terms with their circumstances.

Maggie's West London (pictured) may be situated close to the hustle and bustle of the city, but inside it feels a world away. The brightly coloured building is focused around an open kitchen and surrounded by a small courtyard and flexible annexes. To protect these tranquil spaces – visually and acoustically – from the road and the adjacent Charing Cross Hospital, we wrapped the building in a 4m-high wall and topped it with a floating roof. This allows an abundance of natural light to flow into the centre's main spaces through a ring of clerestory glazing. The centre's columns, ceilings and floors – made from exposed concrete – help moderate the interior temperature and deliver a high-quality acoustic performance. Embodying a sense of home, it's a comfortable environment for visitors and staff alike.

We also helped the charity to export its ethos of sensitive and supportive care outside the UK for the first time. In 2013, we provided pro bono consultancy services for Maggie's in Hong Kong. Set within a Chinese garden, our A-framed timber structure unifies a series of spaces that are flooded with natural light through skylights and storey-height glazed façades. Far removed from the typical sterile hospital setting, it is a sanctuary for patients in search of support and healing.

Building sustainability and seismic resiliency into the hospital environment

By designing inherently environmentally friendly features that will help reduce overall costs for hospital owners, savings can be passed on to patients. In the US, the Kaiser Permanente San Diego Central Hospital, Loma Linda University Medical Center, and Zuckerberg San Francisco General Hospital and Trauma Center each have this aspiration.

The San Diego Central Hospital embraces both technology and the environment to push the boundaries of sustainable hospital design. The use of an active chilled beam mechanical system for the patient rooms – a first for a Californian hospital – helped shave nearly 5% from the mechanical system's energy demand, while also improving thermal comfort for patients. The hospital also uses an innovative new fully LED-based lighting system, which reduces lighting energy demand by 15%. More importantly, controls modulate the white LED lighting system to align with the intensities of daylight and night sky colour temperatures. This colour control helps set the circadian rhythms of patients, which studies have shown leads to shorter hospital stays – a win for both doctors and patients. Combined with a 325kWe solar photovoltaic system and a 650kWe microturbine-based tri-generation plant that also produces 1,500kWth in useful 'waste' heat, the design is projected to save more than 40% in annual energy costs compared with baseline hospitals. It will stand alongside the UCH Macmillan Cancer Centre in London (see page 112) as a benchmark for eco-friendly design in healthcare.

In San Francisco, our engineers are rising to the challenge of creating buildings that will withstand a serious earthquake and remain fully operational throughout. At San Francisco General, we constructed the most advanced seismically resistant design currently in existence. To safeguard the city's busiest emergency room and sole trauma centre, we engineered a base-isolated structure. This allows the building to glide 32 inches in any direction, shielding it from the impact of an earthquake. It's a design that saved 3,000 US tons of steel compared with traditional seismic-design systems, a saving for both material sustainability and construction costs.

At the Loma Linda in California, we are designing a resilient 1.1m square foot acute care trauma centre, with both adult and children's hospitals fit for the modern age. Combining the lessons learned from San Diego Central and San Francisco General, and using advanced analysis tools, we are working with the client and the state of California to develop an advanced base-isolated structural design that exceeds current minimum regulatory standards. This will address significant seismic conditions while reducing the anticipated downtime for the hospital in the immediate aftermath of a major earthquake. Given California's ongoing drought, our civil and plumbing engineers designed low-impact stormwater systems to infiltrate rainwater back into the ground, as well as low-flow plumbing fixtures to reduce potable water consumption by over 35%.

Our innovations are now being adapted by other hospitals to help ensure resiliency and sustainability for people around the world.

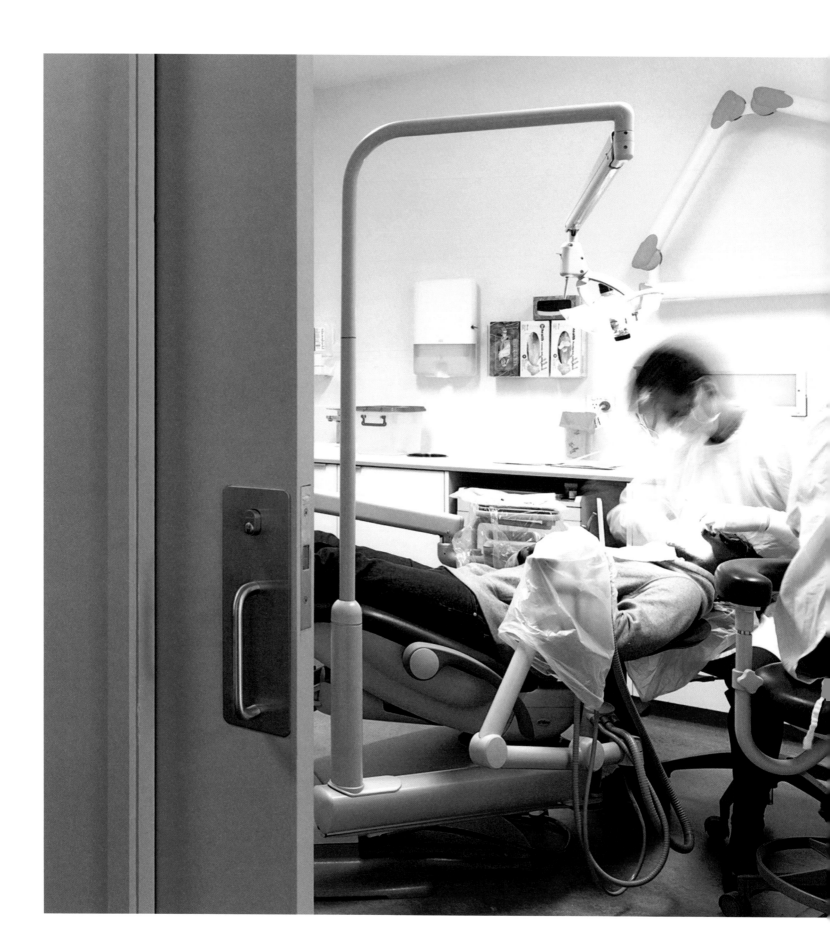

Empowering marginalised communities

Our expertise has helped build and improve hospitals all around the world. In Australia, we have taken on much greater healthcare challenges to provide better services to marginalised communities across the country.

Indigenous Australians suffer disproportionately from chronic diseases such as diabetes and cancer. There are many contributing factors, but the lack of adequate healthcare facilities located in the areas of greatest need is paramount.

We managed the Capital Works Programme for the Office for Aboriginal and Torres Strait Islander Health. This was a programme to improve primary health outcomes within these communities by building and upgrading 200 health centres across the country. We managed the design and delivery of these centres, with project managers and architects ensuring that the resulting buildings were durable, locally sustainable, culturally appropriate and environmentally sensitive.

Key to our success was the active participation of the medical services and the communities they represented. By listening to healthcare providers, community leaders and representative organisations, we were able to ensure that facilities were appropriate to Indigenous Australians' needs. Giving people a voice? That's a step towards empowerment that is healthy for us all.

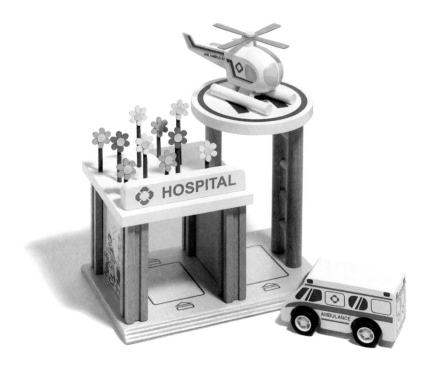

Caring for children

In Dublin, at Our Lady's Children's Hospital, Crumlin, we designed a new paediatric intensive care unit (PICU) and relocated the wounds unit to accommodation underneath the PICU building. Constructed deep within the live hospital complex, the site was constrained by buildings on three sides. This project used the latest methods of offsite prefabrication and fast-track site assembly to minimise disruption and risk to adjacent occupied wards and treatment areas. As with much of our healthcare work, temporary closure was not an option.

We provided all the mechanical and electrical design work for the new 17-bed unit, which includes five single rooms, four passively pressurised isolation suites, an 8-bay observation suite and support facilities. The close relationship developed with hospital staff and patients over this time ensured that the end result met their needs.

We are also consultants for another children's hospital, just 2km away. The National Paediatric Hospital Project is the most significant capital investment in healthcare ever undertaken in Ireland – and it has all been designed to cater for the full spectrum of patients, from babies to young adults.

Spaces and systems are designed to work for patients, families and staff, with wayfinding and orientation simplified and different areas clearly distinguishable from each other. The mechanical and electrical systems will provide resilient, energy-efficient and sustainable systems to support the delivery of clinical excellence. For the first time, automated goods vehicles will be used in an Irish hospital to manage movement of goods and waste.

When it is completed in 2020, the hospital will feature a variety of spaces to create a child-friendly environment that promotes wellbeing and recovery, including a therapeutic rooftop garden, where children can forget about the concerns of the world below.

A new symbol for a new South Africa

Johannesburg's Constitutional Court is much more than just a building. As the first major project built by the post-apartheid government, it is a unifying symbol for the values of new democracy.

With this social purpose in mind, the building actively encourages people to enter and interact. Much of the façade was developed to contain artistic elements, such as the louvres that spin when people touch them. A large part of the court acts as a dedicated gallery space. That sensitivity to the local environment fed into our climate control strategy. By harnessing Johannesburg's climate of extremes – very hot during the day, very cold during the night – we used rock storage to develop passive heating and cooling strategies for the building.

The Constitutional Court set the standard for government and municipal buildings in South Africa, being 'green' before environmental impact ratings were in use. It stands not only as a court, but as a piece of architecture that celebrates the dignity and transparency enshrined within South Africa's constitution.

Enriching education

This is a school like no other. Our work for the Dalai Lama's Drukpa Trust charity, to build the Druk Padma Karpo School (formerly the Druk White Lotus School), took us to one of the most remote locations in the world.

Sitting at an altitude of 3,500m, the Ladakh region in northern India is a high-altitude desert. Temperatures range from 30°C in summer to -30°C in winter. There is risk of earthquakes, and water is scarce. We combined local knowledge, materials, workers and volunteers from our firm with 'simple-smart' cutting-edge technology to engineer a sustainable and safe school for this extreme environment. The timber-framed structure can withstand tremors, water onsite is sourced from melted snow, the toilets don't require water and passive solar heating converts sunlight to thermal energy – even in winter. In 2008, the first stage of a state-of-the-art micro-grid solar power system was installed, using photovoltaic panels to generate electricity and provide lighting.

The school opened in 2001, with the final phase due to complete in 2017. It provides more than 650 children with a high-quality, modern education based on Tibetan Buddhism, maintaining their rich cultural traditions.

Home from home

After Japan's 2011 earthquake and tsunami, communities were left devastated. Through small-scale interventions, architectural charity Home-for-All is bringing a sense of pride back to these broken communities. We worked to deliver one of these spaces in the coastal city of Sōma: a place where adults could gather and children play freely, without concern for background radiation.

The indoor park we created together with the architects is covered by a distinctive roof made from Japanese larch, a 100% renewable and cost-effective material. The park's 3-way weave lattice roof resembles a traditional Japanese straw hat, and works to protect children from the sun. Playful columns support the roof and, in a nod to the local trees, feature owls and squirrels sitting on the branches. It is a space where the families of Sōma can truly feel at home.

Total Design for a changing world

The concept of Total Design has always been at the heart of our firm. But what of the future? As a firm we continually adapt to the challenges posed by a changing world. Globalisation impacts on businesses, nations and decision-makers in ever new ways. Conversely, the demand for hyper-localisation, where needs are met at an almost personal scale, is now an expectation. And as we move into an age that is increasingly digital, innovative and connected, we believe that Ove's founding principles continue to position us to take on these challenges and create value. We strive for design work of quality that is done as well as it can be done, that is socially useful and where design decisions have been considered by integrated teams.

"Total Design has its most exciting impacts when the entire team is given the space to collaborate, think and swap ideas openly at the very start of the design process."

Rob Leslie-Carter, Programme and Project Management, London

What of the future?

Ove was engineer and philosopher, combining thinking with doing. He envisioned an industry that gave equal weight to, and drew upon, the combined strengths of each discipline to produce great work – an idea once deemed radical. In bringing together disparate disciplines, flattening professional hierarchies and fostering a collaborative spirit across teams, his philosophy inspires us to maintain an innovative and imaginative spirit. And it's one that continually renews itself as we respond to the needs of the present day.

We are making increasing use of digital technology, taking advantage of the power of big data, transforming our business and always refining our approach. Arup takes a lead in the digital built environment, demonstrated by our development of simulation technologies such as SoundLab (see pages 23–24) and MassMotion (see page 62), and in how we push the boundaries of building information modelling (BIM) (see opposite).

Powered by technology, the scope, scale and complexity of our work has grown. Projects such as city masterplans (see pages 46–52) constitute a multitude of >

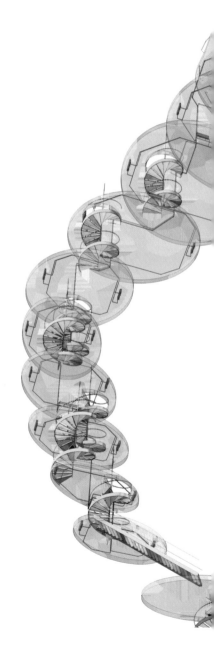

ProjectOVE demonstrates the value of working across silos. This demonstration of a building information modelling (BIM) project uses the most advanced techniques to create a multidisciplinary building model. It is based on the human body and comprises architecture, structure, mechanical ductwork and pipework, and electrical components. BIM can be hugely beneficial in improving information flow and knowledge-sharing among different stakeholders.

127

"In my field of big infrastructure, Total Design is the only goal – what matters most is the outcome for society."

Tim Chapman, Infrastructure Design Consultant, London

interconnected systems, and require sensitivity to both the immediate and wider social, economic and public contexts. We continue to take this 'system-thinking' approach, which enables us to propose deeper-seated, more fundamental solutions rather than partial or piecemeal answers. One such example was our proposal to change the route of HS1 in London so that it fed into King's Cross via Stratford, rather than Waterloo. This far-sighted solution unlocked economic potential for the London 2012 Olympics, and in the surrounding region, from Stratford to the Lower Lee Valley (see page 30).

The need for this level of thinking and foresight is continually growing. Across the world, city resilience is an issue that clients and other decision-makers are beginning to engage with. There is growing awareness that in responding to the emerging connections between social stability, economics, natural threats and the built environment, joined-up thinking is vital. And in tackling global issues such as climate change, our drive to approach problems and solutions collaboratively and holistically becomes invaluable (see page 96). >

The WeatherShift™ tool uses data from the Intergovernmental Panel on Climate Change to project future climate conditions, allowing mechanical engineers to design to those specifications. It means designers are no longer thinking purely about climate within the context of here and now, but are able to provide a solution that will remain relevant over the longer term.

What if a building could organically power itself? Together with other bio-engineering specialists, we built the world's first house with a bio-reactive algae façade in Hamburg. Circulating through 129 nutrient-fed glass panels fixed to the building's south-facing walls, the algae absorb sunlight and the carbon produced by combustion in the building's plant room. This process produces heat, and the algae themselves can be converted into biomass once harvested. Heat and biomass are transported via a closed loop system to the building's energy management centre to be used for power and heat generation. This experiment represents another step on the road towards zero-energy and zero-carbon buildings.

"After delivering a project the end user should actually feel the 'Total Design' and that every part of it was thought holistically."

Francesca Coppa, Acoustic Engineer, Berlin

Bringing disciplines together generates transformative leaps and makes them credible, tangible and deliverable. Embedding sustainability in the new built environment is the kind of challenge that requires precisely this multidimensional thinking. New design, engineering and construction concepts, such as the 'circular economy' where we increasingly build with reuse in mind, represent challenging breaks with tradition. Total Design allows us to unpick and rethink the logic of a linear approach, and in this it is the perfect guiding philosophy to achieve such ambitious new goals.

The true value of the built environment is the human experience it ultimately fosters. Rather than taking things in isolation, Total Design means we never lose sight of this social dimension. People-centred design must consider both ideas and their subsequent effects, if it is to be successful and socially valuable.

Internally, the values of collaboration, experimentation and innovation are also embedded in how we support, train and develop our people. At Arup University, from graduates to senior directors, our members are supported with career-long training and development courses, >

"Total Design is not stopping at the first solution that works but looking to refine the solution to something that is elegant and simple."

Alisdair McGregor, Sustainable Design Consultant, San Francisco

building awareness, and knowledge, of new ideas and techniques. This concentration on breadth of learning is our response to a built environment that is as much a world of ideas as it is physical buildings.

We set up Arup University to fund and pioneer foresight and research into issues facing the world around us. It sparks conversations, hosts lectures and publishes papers, ensuring our industry is constantly learning, rethinking and, ultimately, innovating. In this way, Total Design continues to refresh itself, creating a design and engineering ecosystem fit for the 21st century and beyond.

Today, we are both a breeding ground for new ideas and a highly respected maker of the modern world. To embody true design excellence, engineering must be more than the sum of its parts. Our philosophy continues to prove its relevance and value to the built environment and its changing needs through the value it places on collaboration, innovation and social utility. Taken together, these principles represent our path forward. We are certain that whatever comes next, Total Design will be instrumental in helping to shape a better world.

WikiHouse 4.0 is an open-source approach to building design that allows people to download, digitally manufacture and assemble their own home, without prior construction knowledge. Emphasising knowledge-sharing and the democratisation of the design and construction, it taps into the question of how digital platforms, crowdsourcing and open-source technologies are reshaping the future of the built environment.

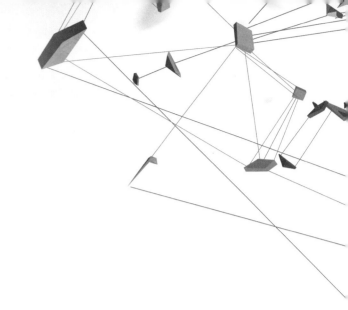

Into the future

We asked Arup colleagues around the world to share their thoughts on how they approach Total Design in their work, and how Total Design improves project outcomes, produces a better built environment and shapes a better world. Here, in a snapshot of their answers, we show how Total Design continues to be relevant.

"To me, Total Design is about the practice of holistic thinking and implementation to create something better and more satisfying. Lateral design-thinking on the basis of sound and innovative technical knowledge is paramount, as is the ability to bring in all of the players at the right time – often on a whim or an idea, listen to everyone and accept exploring ideas that may differ from experience and convention. Sometimes the best ideas come from the uncluttered thoughts of youth, other disciplines, architects, artists and industrial designers, builders, trade contractors, processes or the exploration of new materials and manufacturing techniques outside of our direct sphere. This keeps us fresh, on our toes, and full of a desire to be inspired.

Total Design is also about accepting the risk of failure along the way – to implement it you must bare all and be prepared to challenge, refine and have the will to be better or improve every time. It may be the best of all disciplines or it may be the singular idea absolutely refined that makes a difference. Above all, it must be of value to society and delivered with elegance."
Andrew Johnson, Structural Engineer, Sydney

"My very first design meeting was on a multidisciplinary residential project in London with Foster + Partners. We were still developing the scheme and I was struck by how the discussion constantly skipped between disciplines, from structure to acoustics to architecture to ventilation: an early lesson that the best design for one discipline is not necessarily the best solution for the project. I have tried to follow that ethos ever since."
Chas Pope, Structural Engineer, Beijing

"We are engineers and seek to do, but we should first listen to clients, to colleagues and even to friends and family. A diverse range of perspectives enables us to challenge conventional thinking and create great solutions. On T2 Dublin, we spent time early in the project working with the client team to develop our joint approach. Neither we nor they imposed ideas but we worked collaboratively, putting the project at the forefront of our mind, and this influenced all that followed."
Dervilla Mitchell, Aviation Business Leader, London

"Total Design inspired my development of a 'customer methodology' to operationalise a people focus. By thinking of the transport hub as a product and understanding the needs of all its customers, including the non-travellers, I found I could get beyond the entrenched positions and design and operational approaches that most engineers, architects and planners took to these projects. For me, Total Design is rooted in people – putting people at the centre of planning and design is both the integrating factor and the source of the ideas that define it.

Total Design makes us think about, and strive for, the complete outcome: places that enrich people's lives and where the whole is much greater than the sum of its parts. The post-quake rebuild of Christchurch provided an opportunity to reimagine the city, as well as a challenge to deliver buildings and infrastructure that would give people confidence about returning to the city, but support the city's rebirth."
Brian R. Smith, Transport Planner, Sydney

"Quality is not only defined by the excellence of individual parts. It is achieved through the careful consideration of all aspects of a system. Total Design must involve a broad range of disciplines and stakeholders, and achieve a working environment that supports shared thinking, knowledge exchange and critical review. By considering various viewpoints, we can converge on a design that is better tailored to its environment."
Josef Hargrave, Foresight Consultant, London

"I see Total Design in the way Arup approaches the topic of quality and excellence. How does Arup design the continuous development of its people to be and remain the best? We do this by looking into the future to understand trends, by carrying out our own research and developing our own tools, by connecting people in skill networks to share their knowledge, and by providing training and learning opportunities, using both internal champions and external experts."
Katharina Schwarz, Arup University, Amsterdam

"For me, Total Design starts with an appreciation of your client's objectives, an understanding of the intended 'end game' for a project, and respecting the co-designers and other stakeholders you are working with. When you wrap your head around these variables, you're empowered to have informed conversations with others to deliver better service and, when needed, influence your client to make design decisions that will have more positive effects on the community and environment. We cannot control all parts of a project, but appreciation of Total Design allows us to help shape better outcomes."

Dr Ryan Falconer, Transportation Consultant, Canada

"It's identifying and using the simple opportunity; the small-yet-obvious step to improved application of engineering; to learn from the past and apply in the future. Those opportunities that help bring different people, skills, experience and techniques together (inside and outside of Arup) and deliver a greater technical solution or reduce sustainable impact. It encourages us to think about design, to do what is required, and avoid building what is not needed, using the design process as an opportunity to develop the best possible solution. Questioning the status quo from the outset: 'Is there a better way?', we look to improve on what we do and so we must learn, and to learn, we must question 'why?'.

This is the approach we adopted on Q9 Quartermile (Edinburgh). We proved we could step away from the norm and design, build and protect a structure from fire that was appropriate for the use and arrangement of that building. We used information developed by others to do this. We then shared our learning with others. We avoided adding to the building what wasn't needed."

**Philip Close and Hugh McNamara,
Fire Engineers, Edinburgh**

"Understanding a project's urban and development context is central to my interpretation of Total Design in 2016. Over the past year, I've worked on sustainability, building retrofit and urban design projects in downtown Johannesburg – a challenging, complex and in some ways contradictory site. Issues of sociopolitics, demographic economics and migration inform downtown Jo'burg's urban fabric, which is a site of both opportunity and risk. In order for our projects to succeed in this context, we've learnt to unpack these tangled issues and take on the perspectives of historians, sociologists and development economists. By doing this, we can create socially responsive and responsible interventions that are mindful of both the city and the citizen."
Pulane Mpotokwane, Graduate Architect, Johannesburg

"Total Design represents the integrated intersect among the built, natural and social worlds. It is the careful consideration of the synergies among those and optimising solutions within that. Our climate resilience work at Partners Healthcare is reflective of that approach. It is focused on translating the uncertainty of climate change into resilient solutions that will ensure the continued operation of critical healthcare facilities during extreme events, and therefore the wellbeing of the populations which they serve."
Lisa C. Dickson, Climate Risk and Resiliency Consultant, Boston

"Total Design is not just about the design of a product, or even a building with all its parts being considered as one. It's about the role of these structures in society, the needs they solve and the value they bring. It's no longer enough to create holistic solutions on a building scale – we have to zoom out and consider their role in the bigger context. When all the elements in society are considered as part of a system, we can make them work together and come up with smarter and more sustainable solutions. This, in my view, is the basis of the 'circular city' and, hopefully, our new future."
Salome Galjaard, Product Designer, Amsterdam

"Openness to innovation can deliver something special. Design solutions are not found in linear fashion; rather, they unfold from repeated reworking of ideas, until holistic approaches are established by the team as a whole. Done well – as well as it can be – the built project has elegance and simplicity, delighting users and viewers alike."
Sean Clarke, Business Management Consultant, Cork

"Total Design is more than multidisciplinary engineering. It means that intelligent thought and loving care must underpin every participant's actions on a project. As design integrator on MCB in Mauritius and the IFC office in Ghana, I spent most of my time communicating internally within the Arup team and externally to collaborators, clients and contractors. I wasn't designing slabs, façades or services, but crafting correspondence, hosting workshops and capturing decisions in meetings. In each of these activities, I targeted the optimum blend of technical clarity, team unity, client comfort and project momentum. These were my Total Design criteria."
Susan Snaddon, Planning and Development, Johannesburg

Credits

Cover
Photography: RIBA Collections

Ove Arup

Sydney Opera House, p8
Photography: © Robert Baudin for Hornibrook Ltd.
Courtesy Australian Air Photos

Sir Ove Arup, p10
Photography: Godfrey Argent, National Portrait Gallery,
London

Kingsgate Footbridge, p10–11
Photography: Colin Westwood; De Burgh Galwey,
Architectural Review

Penguin Pool, p12
Photography: © ZSL

Pier Head Fenders (Baker System)
Mulberry Harbour, p13
Photography: Corbis

Brynmawr Rubber Factory, p14
Photography: De Burgh Galwey

Jack Zunz with Ove Arup, p14
Photography: courtesy of Arup

Hidden hand of the engineer

Menil Collection Museum, p16–17
Photography: MenilMtg; © Fondazione Renzo Piano, Via
Rubens, 29 – 16158 Genova, Italy +39-010-691378;
Richard Bryant

Centre Pompidou, p18
Photography: Luciano Mortula/Alamy

Lloyd's Building, p19 & p21
Illustration: Peter James Field
Photography: Prisma Bildagentur AG/Alamy

Richard Rogers, p20
Photography: BeaubourgTrio_240x

The Leadenhall Building, p21
Photography: Daniel Imade/courtesy of Arup

Snape Maltings Concert Hall, p22
Photography: Nick Jones/Suffolk County Music Service

Arup SoundLab, p23
Photography: Andre Costantini/courtesy of Arup

Sound form: visual representation of sound, p24
Illustration: Justin Metz/Debut art

National Taichung Theater, p26
Photography: TIAA/courtesy of Arup

Osaka Maritime Museum, p28
Photography: Katsuhisa Kida

Transforming cities

Three decades of rail revolution, p30
Illustration: Terence Eduarte/YCN

Stratford City Masterplan, p31
Illustration: Terence Eduarte/YCN

Crossrail, p32
Photography: Robby Whitfield © Crossrail Ltd

King's Cross Station, p32
Illustration: Peter James Field

Hudson River Park, p34–36
Photography: Hudson River Park Trust; iStock

Map of Manhattan, p37
Photography: iStock

Hong Kong skyline, p38
Photography: Bloomberg/Getty Images

Salford Docks Development, p40
Photography: courtesy of Arup; Jonathan Webb

Global urbanisation

China Central Television (CCTV) Headquarters, p42
Photography: DuKai/Getty Images

Building tall across the decades, p43
Graphic: courtesy of Arup

Shanghai, p44
Photography: Manfred Gottschalk/Getty Images

Dongtan, p46
Photography: Shanghai Industrial Investment (Holdings) Co
Ltd; courtesy of Arup

City of Tshwane Inner City Regeneration Project, p48
Photography: courtesy of Arup

Seychelles Strategic Masterplan & Economic
Study, p49
Photography: courtesy of Wardour

Marina Bay, p50
Photography: courtesy of Arup

Msheireb (regeneration of Inner Doha designated
district), p52
Photography: courtesy of Wardour

People on the move

Terminal 3, Beijing Capital International
Airport, p54
Photography: DigitalGlobe/ScapeWare3d/Getty Images

London Stansted Airport – New Terminal Building, p56
Photography: courtesy of Arup

Luggage labels, p58
Photography: Pixeleyes; Wardour

Kansai International Airport Terminal Building, p60
Photography: Y Kinumaki; courtesy of Arup

Terminal 5, JFK International Airport, New York, p61
Photography: Randy Duchaine/Alamy

Crowd of people from above, p62
Photography: iStock

Hong Kong Metro, p65
Photography: Cultura RM Exclusive/Alan Graf/Getty Images

Second Avenue Subway, p66
Photography: Richard Barnes/OTTO

Øresundbroen Link, p68–69
Photography: Tom Nagy/Gallerystock
Illustration: Peter James Field

Kylesku Bridge, p70
Photography: Craig Easton/Gallerystock

Millennium Footbridge, p72
Photography: Ben Stansall/Getty Images

Project information

181 Fremont Tower, p99
Designed for: Jay Paul Company
Designed with: Heller Manus Architects

1.8, p90
Designed for: Janet Echelman and presented by Artichoke
Designed with: Janet Echelman

30 St Mary Axe, p43
Designed for: Swiss Reinsurance Co (UK) Ltd
Designed with: Foster + Partners

Adelaide Desalination Plant Transfer Pipeline System, p100
Designed for: McConnell Dowell/Built Environs JV
Designed with: Logicamms

Angel of the North, p92
Designed for: Gateshead Metropolitan Borough Council
Designed with: Antony Gormley

Bangkok Wastewater Phase 2 – Yannawa, p100
Designed for: Samsung-Lotte-CEC JV
Designed with: Babcock Water Engineering Ltd; Epsilon Architects

Beddington Zero Energy Development, p106
Designed for: Peabody Trust
Designed with: Bill Dunster Architects

BioBuild – Biocomposites for Building Applications, p107
Designed for: European Commission
Designed with: GXN Architects

Brynmawr Rubber Factory, p14
Designed for: Enfield Cable Works Ltd
Designed with: Architects Co-partnership Ltd; Enfield Cable Works Ltd

California Academy of Sciences, p84
Designed for: California Academy of Sciences
Designed with: Renzo Piano Building Workshop Srl; Gordon H Chong & Associates

Canton Tower, p43
Designed for: Guangzhou New TV Tower Construction Co Ltd
Designed with: Information Based Architecture

Central Plaza, p43
Designed for: Sun Hung Kai Properties Ltd; Ryoden Property Development Co Ltd; Sino Land Co Ltd
Designed with: Ng Chun Man & Associates

Central to Eveleigh Urban Renewal, p48
Designed for: UrbanGrowth NSW
Designed with: Grimshaw Architects

Centre Pompidou, p18, p20
Designed for: Etablissement Public Du Centre Beaubourg
Designed with: Piano & Rogers

Channel Tunnel Rail Link (now known as High Speed 1), p30, p128
Designed for: London & Continental Railways Engineering (LCR)
Designed with: Rail Link Engineering (RLE) a JV of Arup; Halcrow; Systra

CHCH Earthquake Assessment, p98
Designed for: New Zealand Earthquake Commission (EQC)
Designed with: Tonkin & Taylor

China Central Television (CCTV) Headquarters, p41, p43
Designed for: China Central Television (CCTV)
Designed with: Office for Metropolitan Architecture

China World Tower, p43
Designed for: China World Trade Centre Company Ltd
Designed with: Skidmore Owings & Merrill LLP

China Zun, p43
Designed for: CITIC Group Corporation
Designed with: Kohn Pedersen Fox Associates

Citi Data Centre, p104
Designed for: Citigroup Inc

City of Tshwane Inner City Regeneration Project, p48
Designed for: City of Tshwane

Commerzbank Tower, p43
Designed for: Commerzbank
Designed with: Foster + Partners

Constitutional Court, p121
Designed for: Johannesburg Development Agency
Designed with: Sibanye Consulting Engineers

Crossrail, p30, p32, p64
Designed for: Crossrail Ltd
Designed with: Arup/Atkins JV (AAJV)

CTF Finance Centre, p43
Designed for: New World Development Co Ltd
Designed with: Kohn Pedersen Fox Associates; Leigh & Orange

Dhajji Dewari report, p98
Designed with: UN-Habitat, Pakistan; ConservationTech; Frederick Hertz; Kashmir Earthquake Relief (KER); University of Engineering and Technology, Peshawar

Dongtan Eco-city, p46
Designed for: Shanghai Industrial Investment Corporation

Druk Padma Karpo School, p122
Designed for: Drukpa Kargyud Trust
Designed with: Duncan Woodburn & Jonathan Rose

Dubai Airport, Terminal 3 Operational Readiness, p59, p61
Designed for: Dubai Civil Aviation

East River Waterfront, p37
Designed for: New York City Economic Development Corporation
Designed with: Daniel Frankfurt (later HDR) (joint venture); SHoP Architects

Emley Moor Television Tower, p43
Designed for: Independent Television Authority
Designed with: Tileman & Co Ltd

The Francis Crick Institute (formerly UKCMRI), p89
Designed for: UK Centre For Medical Research & Innovation
Designed with: Hellmuth Obata & Kassabaum Inc

Frick Chemistry Laboratory, p88
Designed for: Princeton University
Designed with: Payette Associates Inc; Hopkins Architects Limited

Fulton Center, p62
Designed for: Metropolitan Transportation Authority; New York City Transit
Designed with: Grimshaw Architects; Page Ayres Cowley Architects; HDR | Daniel Frankfurt

Gardens by the Bay, p50
Designed for: National Parks Board, Singapore
Designed with: CPG Consultants; Grant Associates; Wilkinson Eyre Architects

Glyndebourne Opera House, p25
Designed for: Glyndebourne Productions Ltd
Designed with: Michael Hopkins & Partners

Gold Coast Light Rail, p64
Designed for: Queensland State Government
Designed with: McConnell Dowell as part of GoldLinQ Consortium (also comprising Keolis; Downer EDI; Plenary Group; Bombardier; and ERM)

Goldin Finance 117, p43
Designed for: Tianjin High-tech New Star Property Development Co Ltd
Designed with: P&T Architects

Green Engage Online, p101
Designed for: InterContinental Hotels Group

Project information continued

National Paediatric Hospital Project, p120
Designed for: National Paediatric Hospital Development Board and Children's Hospital Group
Designed with: BDP; O'Connel Mahon Architects

National Taichung Theater, p26
Designed for: Taichung City Government
Designed with: Toyo Ito & Associates

Nepal earthquake: various projects, p98
Designed with: World Bank; Save the Children Nepal; Americares; NSET; ASF; Splash; EEFIT

Northeast Asia Trade Tower, p43
Designed for: New Songdo City Development LLC
Designed with: Kohn Pedersen Fox Associates PC

OCBC Bank, p43
Designed for: OCBC Centre Pte Ltd
Designed with: I M Pei; BEP Partnership

Office of Aboriginal and Torres Strait Islander Health – Primary Health Care Access Program, p118
Designed for: Department of Health & Ageing

One Central Park, p43
Designed for: Frasers Property
Designed with: Ateliers Jean Nouvel

Øresundbroen Link, p68
Designed for: Øresundskonsortiet
Designed with: Georg Rotne Architect MAA; Setec Travaux Publics & Industriels; Gimsing & Madsen AS; ISC Consulting Engineers AS

Osaka Maritime Museum, p25, p28
Designed for: Osaka Port & Harbour Bureau
Designed with: Paul Andreu Architects; Tohata Architects & Engineers

Oslo Opera House/Nytt Operahus, p24
Designed for: Statsbygg
Designed with: Snohetta As

Our Lady's Children's Hospital, Crumlin – Paediatric Intensive Care Unit (PICU), p120
Designed for: Our Lady's Children's Hospital, Crumlin
Designed with: Scott Tallon Walker; John Sisk & Son Ltd

Penguin Pool, p12
Designed for: Zoological Society of London
Designed with: Berthold Lubetkin; Tecton Ltd

Pier A, p37
Designed for: Battery Park City Authority
Designed with: H3 Hardy Collaboration Architecture

Pier A Plaza Renovation, p37
Designed for: New York City Economic Development Corporation; Battery Park City Authority
Designed with: Rogers Marvel Architects

Pier 55, Hudson River Park, p37
Designed for: Hudson River Park Trust
Designed with: Heatherwick Studio; Mathews Nielsen Landscape Architects

Pier Head Fenders (Baker System) Mulberry Harbour, p13
Designed for: Ministry of Defence

Priscilla and Mark Zuckerberg San Francisco General Hospital and Trauma Center, p116
Designed for: City of San Francisco
Designed with: Fong & Chan

Raffles City, Hangzhou, p43
Designed for: CapitaLand (China) Investment Co Ltd
Designed with: UN Studio

Ravenspurn North Concrete Gravity Substructure, p103
Designed for: Hamilton Brothers Oil & Gas Ltd

Robert F Wagner Jr Park, p37
Designed for: Battery Park City Authority
Designed with: Machado and Silvetti Associates, Inc; Hanna/Olin

Rosherville PV, p101
Designed for: Eskom Renewables Unit
Designed with: Basil Reed Matomo

Sabiha Gökçen Airport Istanbul, New Terminal Building, p58
Designed for: GMR/Limak/MAHB Consortium
Designed with: Dogan Tekeli

The Sainsbury Laboratory, p86
Designed for: University of Cambridge
Designed with: Stanton Williams Ltd

Sainsbury Wellcome Centre, p87
Designed for: UCL Properties Ltd
Designed with: Ian Ritchie Architects

Salford Docks Development, p40
Designed for: City of Salford
Designed with: Shepheard Epstein Hunter

Second Avenue Subway, p66
Designed for: New York City Transit Authority
Designed with: AECOM

Seychelles Strategic Plan, p49
Designed for: Abu Dhabi Urban Planning Council and Government of Seychelles

The Shard, p43
Designed for: Sellar Property Group
Designed with: Renzo Piano Building Workshop Srl

Singapore Flyer, p50
Designed for: Singapore Flyer Pte Ltd + Melchers Project Management
Designed with: Kisho Kurokawa Architect & Associates; DP Architects

Singapore Metro, p64
Designed for: Singapore Land Transport Authority

Singapore Sports Hub, p76
Designed for: Dragages Singapore Pte Ltd
Designed with: Dp Architects Pte Ltd

Sir Thomas White Building, St John's College, p82
Designed for: St John's College Oxford

Smart Park Strategy, p81
Designed for: London Legacy Development Corporation

Snape Maltings Concert Hall, p22
Designed for: Aldeburgh Festival of Music & The Arts

SolarLeaf Algae Façade, p130
Designed for: International Building Exhibition Hamburg (IBA 2013)
Designed with: Strategic Science Consult (SSC); Colt International

Stratford City Masterplan, p31
Designed for: Chelsfield/Stanhope
Designed with: Fletcher Priest Architects

Support to the Office of Housing Recovery Operations, p99
Designed for: New York City Office of Housing Recovery Operations; US Federal Emergency Management Agency
Designed with: Architecture Research Office; ATCS; AECOM

Sydney Opera House, p8
Designed for: New South Wales Department of Public Works
Designed with: Jorn Utzon; Hall Todd & Littlemore; Hanson & Todd Pty Ltd; New South Wales Government; Rudder Littlemore & Rudder Pty Ltd; Stephen George & Partners; C P Weatherburn

Taoyuan International Airport (Taipei) Terminal 3, p59, p61
Designed for: Taoyuan International Airport Corporation Ltd
Designed with: Rogers Stirk Harbour + Partners; CECI Engineering Consultants, Inc; Taiwan Fei & Cheng Associates

Teardrop Park, Battery Park City, p37
Designed for: Battery Park City Authority
Designed with: Michael Van Valkenburgh Associates Inc

Terminal 5, JFK International Airport, New York, p59, p61–62
Designed for: JetBlue Airways Corporation
Designed with: Gensler

The Arup Design Book is produced and published
for Arup by Wardour

For Arup
Arup Design Book Publishing Board
Tristram Carfrae, Mark Bidgood, Malcolm Smith, Nigel Tonks

Karim Klaus Emara, Chief Marketing Officer
David Boreham, Project Director
Karen Hanson, Project Manager

For Wardour
The core team was led by Claire Oldfield, who also took
the editorial lead, Ben Barrett, who took the creative lead,
and account director Georgina Beach. The team included:
Lynn Jones, Dean Buckley, Louise Hewlett and Jane Duru.

Thanks to the writers, editors, researchers and artworkers
who worked alongside the core team and with the wider
production team – there are too many to mention.

Wardour, Drury House, 34–43 Russell Street,
London WC2B 5HA, United Kingdom
+44 (0)20 7010 0999
www.wardour.co.uk

'wardour '

Arup Design Book is printed
by Hampton Printing Limited, Bristol
on FSC certified material.

Arup Design Book
Total Design over time
ISBN no: 978-0953823963

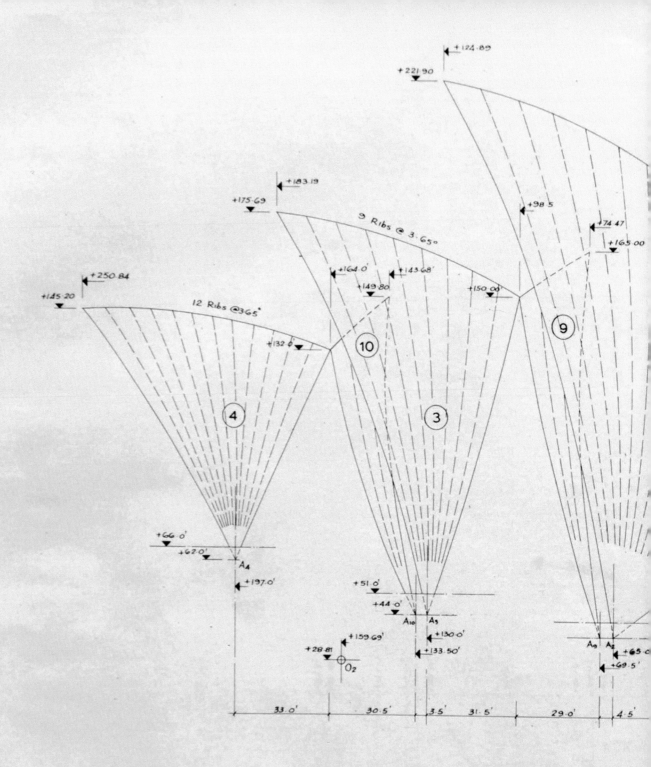

ELEVATION